CASE STUDIES IN ECONOMICS

Projects and Role Playing in Teaching Economics

Other books by C. T. Sandford

Taxing Inheritance and Capital Gains
Economics of Public Finance: An Economic Analysis of
Government Expenditure and Revenue in the United Kingdom
Realistic Tax Reform

Projects and Role Playing in Teaching Economics

C. T. Sandford, M. S. Bradbury and Associates

Macmillan

First published 1971 by
THE MACMILLAN PRESS LTD
London and Basingstoke
Associated companies in New York Toronto
Dublin Melbourne Johannesburg and Madras

SBN 333 10278 9 (hard cover)

Printed in Great Britain by
RICHARD CLAY (THE CHAUCER PRESS) LTD
Bungay, Suffolk

Contents

Preface and Acknowledgements

This book is one of a series on case studies in economics consisting initially of three volumes. A volume on *Principles of Economics* and a companion volume on *Economic Policy* use case studies as illustrations and exercises and are intended to be study and workbooks for students of economics preparing for 'A'-level, first-year degree, H.N.D. and H.N.C. in business studies and professional examinations. This volume is written specifically for teachers and offers guidance on how to prepare case studies, along with examples of projects and role-playing case studies in a form which makes it easy for teachers to adopt them.

The main advantage of the case-study approach is its realism, for a case study is taken to be a detailed examination of an actual or closely simulated economic situation, phenomenon or development from which economic understanding can be gained.

A notable feature of the series is the extent to which the material has been tried out in the classroom and the 'field'. Most of the chapters in *Principles of Economics* and *Economic Policy* have been modified in the light of the comments of the teachers – in secondary schools, colleges of further education, colleges of education, polytechnics and universities – who tested the material with their own students. All the projects and role-playing case studies in this volume (though not necessarily all the variants) have been used in teaching; but it has been thought sensible to indicate modifications which, in the light of experience, the teachers plan to introduce in repeating the exercises, even though at the time of writing they have not yet had the chance to do so.

Our thanks are due to the many students and teachers who, experimenting with some of these case studies, have helped to improve their effectiveness as learning aids. More specifically we wish to thank the Marley Floor Tile Company Ltd for allowing their name to appear at the head of one of the studies and, with representatives of Lloyds Bank, United City Merchants and the Board of Trade, for taking part in it (Chapter 9). We wish also to thank the officials of the Location of Offices

vii

Bureau for help and advice with the case study in Chapter 11. Further, we gratefully acknowledge the permission granted by the editors of the *American Economic Review* to republish, in Chapters 6 and 7, the substance of an article, 'Role Playing in Teaching Economics', by Professor Myron L. Joseph of Carnegie-Mellon University, which appeared in the *A.E.R.*, LV (1965); and by the editors of *Economics*, the journal of the Economics Association, to republish in Chapters 5, 17 and part of 15 modified versions of articles which had previously appeared in that journal.

Having acknowledged debts, we must also indicate liabilities. For surviving blemishes and errors the authors are alone responsible.

C. T. S.
M. S. B.

Introduction

The purpose of this book is simple: it is both to encourage experimentation in the methods of teaching economics and to raise the quality of such experimentation.

The past decade or so has seen many new approaches to teaching and learning in primary schools, rather fewer in secondary schools and probably fewer still in further and higher education. In economics teaching there have been no startling developments like Nuffield mathematics or language laboratories; but anyone in close touch with economics teachers cannot fail to detect a widespread interest in improving teaching method.

The leading role in stimulating this interest in the United Kingdom – by its discussion groups, its journal and its pioneering publications, such as *Teaching Economics* – has been played by the Economics Association. The rapid growth of the Association in recent years is itself a sign of this interest in improving teaching methods. Moreover, in part through the stimulation of the Association, in a quiet way, much useful work has been taking place. There is thus an increased willingness among teachers of economics both to initiate experiments in teaching method and to try out the experiments of others.

One field for experimentation is in the use of case studies in the form of projects and role-playing exercises, and this book assembles examples of such case studies. But the use of case studies has dangers as well as merits; undertaken without adequate preparation and skill they can be worse than useless. This is especially true of the surveys which form a part of most case-study projects; surveys are currently in vogue on a whole range of subjects and they are often lightly embarked upon by teachers who lack the expertise to ensure that they yield meaningful and worth-while results. Worse, flooding the market with incompetent surveys spoils it for the competent. Thus this volume seeks not only to encourage the development of case studies by illustrating how they have been and may be used by practising teachers, but also to provide understanding and practical guidance to help competence keep pace with enthusiasm.

These objectives dictate the structure of the book. Part One deals with methodology. The first chapter is an attempt to analyse the meaning, merits and limitations of the case-study method as applied to economics; it is inevitably tentative because experience is narrowly limited and the literature extremely meagre. The next three chapters consider aspects of surveys – planning and sampling problems, questionnaire construction and interviewing techniques; they do not claim to be comprehensive, but highlight the main issues and provide guidance on further reading. The fifth chapter examines visits and field studies in teaching economics. Then come the case studies themselves, which methodologically fall into three categories: role-playing by students (and sometimes staff); role-playing by experts (the Marley export case, Chapter 9); and projects, generally of a group nature, which are concerned to examine some particular economic problem or area, but where the student is not required to assume a role other than that of student. The dividing line is sometimes a little thin; for example, one of the two cases considered in 'Investing on the Stock Exchange' (Chapter 16) is presented in role-playing, the other in project form; but it would have been possible to present both in either guise. For this reason no attempt has been made to arrange the studies according to this methodological classification. Instead grouping has been roughly according to subject-matter, beginning with micro-topics and proceeding to macro; but no particular significance attaches to the order.

The format of the case-study chapters has been designed to facilitate their use by teachers. Each study starts with a statement of aims; then follows an indication of the student levels for which the study is considered appropriate and the requirements in money, equipment and time needed to undertake it. Next comes a statement of the preparatory work necessary before the study itself is undertaken. Whenever appropriate a subsection is devoted to particular problems of application so that the teacher may anticipate the difficulties. Finally, variants to the study may be indicated to suggest how it might be developed to emphasise points or bring out new ones, or how the same method might be adapted to other aspects of economics.

Deliberately no attempt has been made to keep uniform the level of the studies included; this is a book for teachers, and many of them, in colleges of further education, in colleges of education, polytechnics and universities will be teaching at different levels. Even in secondary schools, economics may be taught at 'O' and 'A' levels and as a general study. Thus it may meet the needs and convenience of many teachers to gather within the same covers case studies at different levels. But there is a further reason. A study designed for one group of students may be capable of adaptation to meet the needs of another group at a different level; the authors have sometimes suggested such modifications, but even where they have not, we hope that the study may occasionally generate an idea which will lead the reader to develop new case-study material to meet his own teaching needs. In these ways we hope that the book may have a creative and perhaps catalytic effect.

Because of the different levels of the case studies, the length of treatment also varies somewhat; we have thought it sensible to allow a fuller treatment of the two most advanced studies (Chapters 12 and 13) so that the methods employed should be fully understood.

For the benefit of overseas readers a rudimentary interpretation of some aspects of the English educational system must be given so that terms used in the text can be understood and related to other educational structures. We hope that we can meet this need without doing too much violence to the sensitivity of English educationists. English secondary education extends from roughly the ages of eleven to 18. The more academic students take examinations known as the General Certificate of Education which is taken at Ordinary ('O') level by students of about sixteen years and at Advanced ('A') level two or three years later. In practice up to ten 'O'-level subjects may be taken and usually three 'A'-level. Performance at 'A' level is the normal means of qualifying for university entrance. Colleges of further education cater for students of fifteen and upwards in a wide variety of subjects at levels varying from school to honours degree. Many studying economics at these colleges will be preparing for examinations for professional qualifications, such as the institutes of secretaries, bankers or chartered accountants, and the majority of students will be part-time. Polytechnics cater for the more advanced of the professional studies and are comparable to universities in the level of most of their work. Some colleges of further education and most polytechnics offer higher national diplomas (H.N.D.) and certificates (H.N.C.) in business studies which include economics. The H.N.D. is obtained by two years' full-time study or on a 'sandwich' basis (in which periods of full-time study alternate with full-time work in industry or commerce); the H.N.C. by part-time study. The level of these qualifications is a little lower than that of a degree. Colleges of education are exclusively concerned with the education of teachers, who may take either a three-year course for a certificate in education or a four-year course to a bachelor's degree in education.

In conclusion we wish to add that we invite and welcome comments from teachers who use this and the other two volumes in the series. The gap between aims and achievements, like the gap between teaching and learning, is often very wide and we are concerned to reduce both. We shall be grateful both to those who take the trouble to tell us of imperfections and how we may set about removing them; and also for information on other successful projects and role-playing case studies in economics.

C. T. SANDFORD
M. S. BRADBURY

Part One

Methodology

CHAPTER ONE

The Use of Case Studies in Economics

C. T. Sandford and M. S. Bradbury

The case study is most widely known, and most generally thought of, as a teaching method in business studies in which students simulate the roles of business executives. They are given detailed information about certain aspects of a business, which they discuss, and on which they are expected to make a 'decision' which, if they were not role-playing, would issue in action. The decisions relate to some aspect of a firm's policy such as marketing, investment or labour relations. The data are generally derived from an actual firm, though occasionally imaginary data may be used. The institution most famous for this approach to learning is the Harvard Business School, and Harvard exponents speak of 'The Case Method'.[1]

But, as F. P. G. Whitaker has pointed out, 'There is, of course, no such thing as "The Case Method". There are several kinds of cases and many methods of using them.'[2] Whitaker then proceeds to distinguish six methods of using case studies: cases as examples; cases as exercises; the use of films as cases; cases as projects; cases used to explore a subject; and non-directive teaching by cases. To this somewhat over-lapping list could be added recent developments such as the use of TV cases,[3] tape-recorded material and computer-assisted games.

Perhaps at this point we owe it to the reader to attempt a definition of a case study – although definitions are not easy to

[1] M. P. McNair (ed.), *The Case Method at the Harvard Business School* (New York and London, 1954).

[2] 'The Use of Cases in a University', in *Case Study Practice* (British Institute of Management, Bedford, 1960).

[3] For example, *Hardy Heating Co. Ltd*, a case study in management accounting, first broadcast on B.B.C. 1 and Radio 3 in 1969 and used in conjunction with a text by G. Ray, J. Smith and P. Donaldson, *Hardy Heating Co. Ltd* (B.B.C. Publications, 1968).

3

find in the literature, most writers apparently assuming that case studies do not need to be explicity defined.

WHAT IS A CASE STUDY?

A case study in economics may be defined as the examination of an actual or closely simulated economic problem, situation, event or development. A case study is characterised by being detailed, limited and unified. These features are complementary and the terms are relative: the detail is more than that which would normally be included in a general textbook or a course of lectures appropriate to a particular level; because of that a case study must be limited in its scope, and the unity arises from confining attention to a circumscribed subject-matter with a specified beginning and end. In other words, a case is *specific* to a place, a theme and a time. Cases tend to be 'micro' rather than 'macro' studies – but they do not have to be: a study of budgetary policy or of planning or of movements in interest rates in a particular country over a defined period can reasonably be included within the terms of the definition. The purpose of case studies in economics is to further economic understanding: any case which fails to assist the learning of economic principles or concepts or to make contemporary economic happenings more meaningful is a waste of time.

While, as Whitaker pointed out, there are many ways of using cases, a broad methodological distinction can be made between case studies which are used to illustrate principles and case studies from which principles can be *derived*. Let us examine these two possibilities more fully.

CASE STUDIES AS ILLUSTRATIONS OF PRINCIPLES[1]

The use of case studies in economics has been almost entirely of this first kind. There is a long tradition of including case studies in lectures and textbooks on economics as an adjunct to theory. Ever since Adam Smith illustrated the principle of division of labour by the famous case study of a pin factory, economists have attempted to give concrete illustrations to

[1] The examples in this section are mainly drawn from the other Case Studies books in this series: *Principles of Economics* and *Economic Policy*.

principles by referring to particular cases. The reader or listener is not expected to make his own generalisations from the cases; rather their purpose is to make clearer and more readily acceptable principles that have already been enunciated.

If this use of case studies as illustrations is not new, it can nevertheless be doubted whether it is used enough as a teaching – or rather learning – aid, and whether its value has been sufficiently appreciated. The case study differs from any general illustration from common experience by reason of its realism, the product of its specific and detailed nature. Thus it is *not* a case study to exemplify the effects of changes in interest rates on different kinds of investment simply by saying that the cost of nuclear generation is more affected than the cost of conventional generation because nuclear generation involves a larger proportion of capital charges to running expenses; it *is* a case study to give figures of the cost of nuclear generation and the effect of interest rates on those costs for particular nuclear power stations, which can be compared with actual costs of conventional generation.

The merit of case studies as illustrations is vividness derived from realism. This it is which, if they are well chosen, gives case studies a distinct learning 'edge' over the economic principle presented without example, or with only a generalised illustration. It is one thing to say that, if a country devalues its currency, some exporters may seek to exploit the new market situation by raising prices in terms of their own currency in order to spend more on export promotion from increased unit profits. It is another thing to show that, following the devaluation of sterling by 14 per cent in November 1967, C. and J. Clark Ltd raised sterling prices in all their markets (except Russia) by 8 per cent and used the higher unit profits to support a policy of market penetration by employing their own sales staff instead of commission agents in overseas markets, by the provision of in-stock service and by increased advertising, and then to be able to follow this up by an examination of their export sales figures before and after devaluation. Such a real-world case study gives a student a more enduring recollection of one of the ways devaluation may work, and a fuller appreciation of the complexities of the economic scene – without at the same time so submerging him in detail that he loses sight of the principle that is being illustrated.

5

Another value of the case-study illustration is that the student is brought into contact with the raw material of his subject instead of continually dealing with 'processed' material. In this way, almost imperceptibly, he may imbibe knowledge of the economic environment.

To these features and also to the limitations and dangers of the use of case studies we shall return. For the moment let us examine more closely the opposite conception of the use of case studies: not as illustrations of received theory, but rather as the means by which and from which generalisations can be derived.

Principles Derived from Case Studies

This is the essence of the Harvard Business School method: case studies are not to illustrate principles; rather principles are derived from cases. Out of the study of reality, out of an examination of the detail of particular business problems, emerges the understanding, the wisdom, which permits the making of generalisations and indeed decisions. As Vanderblue and Cragg put it: 'The student must understand the facts of the case and then perform for himself the task of inducing from them one or more principles.'[1]

This kind of 'learning by doing', the essence of business cases, has never been adopted as part of the learning process in economics as distinct from some of the business cases with economic aspects. Putting the point in another way: while not all business schools are as enamoured of this method of using case studies as Harvard, it would be a distinct rarity to find a department of management or business studies in a British university which omitted to make some use of the method. Conversely, it would be a rarity to find an economics department in a British university which did. Why is this? Why have case studies rarely been used in economics as a means of *deriving* principles, while this has been a major use in business studies?

A number of reasons may be hazarded. Economics has a body of developed theory which business studies lacks. Until

[1] Homer B. Vanderblue and Charles I. Cragg, 'The Case Method of Teaching Economics', in C. E. Fraser (ed.), *The Case Method of Instruction* (New York and London, 1931).

6

recent years the emphasis of economics has been on model-building, on deductive rather than empirical methods. Business is concerned with decision-making after regard for a complex of factors which span the academic disciplines. Economics has been concerned to keep itself pure and positive. Economics claims the status of a science where business is more readily recognised as an art. Most practical decisions involve not only economics but other considerations as well – value judgements and political considerations (in the broadest sense); the economist, as a scientist, is concerned to point out the economic implications of alternative courses of action, but to leave the actual decision-making to someone else.

Whatever the reasons may be, the differences are marked; they are seen at their most extreme if we compare not the use of individual case studies but courses of case studies. In the teaching of business administration, it is by no means unusual for a course to consist entirely of case studies. The authors of this chapter can find only one published example of an economics course based entirely on case studies – a first-year course taught by V. R. Fuchs and A. W. Warner at the Columbia University School of General Studies.[1] It was a course in 'Introduction to Economic Analysis' for mature students which sought to train them in fundamentals rather than survey economic ideas over a wide range, and which followed a course of introductory economics. The case-study course was organised around concepts and tools such as demand, supply, equilibrium, elasticity, rather than around policy questions. The cases, as described by the authors, consisted of a variety of illustrative devices varying from simple mathematical problems or collections of statistical data to complex descriptions of real-life problems which called for an economic solution. In arranging the course the attempt was made to proceed from the simple to the more difficult and to enable students to analyse complex situations using the concepts they had previously acquired. The order followed was (1) the nature of economic analysis, (2) demand, (3) supply and cost, (4) equilibrium, (5) elasticity, (6) maximisation and marginal analysis, and (7) aggregate analysis. There were no lectures, each class consisting of dis-

[1] V. R. Fuchs and A. W. Warner, 'The "Case Method" Approach to Teaching Elementary Economics', in K. A. Knopf and J. H. Stauss (eds), *The Teaching of Elementary Economics* (New York, 1960).

cussion of the assigned cases under the guidance of the instructor. The authors concluded from their experience of the case method that economic cases should (i) be brief so as to avoid raising too many issues which would obscure the main points; (ii) conclude with questions to focus attention on the concepts; (iii) afford an opportunity to test the conclusion reached under one set of circumstances by reference to other situations which were, superficially similar; (iv) be drawn from a variety of economic fields; (v) incidentally acquaint the student with the various sources of economic information; (vi) make the student feel that he was acquiring a useful set of tools and at the same time make him realise the limitations of economic data and of the uses to which his analytical techniques might be put.

This course has been outlined fairly fully because of its intrinsic interest for the teacher of economics; but in the context of our argument the crucial factors are that the course *followed* a course of introductory economics and consisted essentially of a variety of *illustrative devices*. Thus, the one example of a course of case studies in economics is primarily concerned with illustrating principles which have already been taught by more traditional methods; it is very different from the case-study courses in business management which seek to provide a basis of fact which will yield its own generalisations.

The differences between economics and business studies are sufficiently real to justify at any rate a marked difference in emphasis in the way case studies are used. Nevertheless, the current trend to empiricism in economics may do something to pull the two approaches nearer or, more specifically, to encourage the use of case studies in economics for purposes additional to illustration, important though that may be. In order to bring out the difference of approach between the use of case studies in business administration and that in economics, it has been useful to distinguish between cases to illustrate principles and cases from which principles may be derived. But we would suggest that, in reality, this dichotomy is overdrawn.

THE PLACE OF CASE STUDIES IN ECONOMICS

Just as, in the development of a science, the processes of deduction and induction, of logical analysis and empirical investigation, are inextricably interconnected, so we cannot separate into completely watertight compartments the procedure of 'illustrating' the generalisations of economic analysis by reference to real-world cases and that of deriving economic principles from an examination of cases. Illustrating by cases is a crude form of empirical testing or verification; as such there will be times when the facts of a case study may lead to doubts about the validity of the generalisation they purport to illustrate, and to some consequential modification of that generalisation. While case studies in economics help to give body to principles previously learnt, they also constitute *part* of the students' experience of real economic situations; on the basis of a learning theory developed from Piaget and Bruner, ability to manipulate abstract concepts rests mainly on an appreciation of the relationship between these concepts and concrete situations.[1] If the learning process is viewed in this light, then case studies assume a place in the learning of economics which is integral rather than peripheral. Case studies in economics illustrate principles, demonstrate applications and promote generalisations as part of the total learning process. While the differences between the use of case studies in business administration and in economics cannot be wholly eliminated because of the different nature and purpose of the disciplines, as *part* of the learning process in economics case studies can be used in a way not dissimilar from that of business studies cases; and some of the advantages claimed for this teaching method in business studies may be gained in economics. This similarity is seen most clearly in the use of case studies, as in this volume, as role-playing exercises and projects, although much that is said below, both of the merits and limitations of case studies, applies also to their use as illustrations.

The Merits of Case Studies

First and essentially, the role-playing or project case study is a form of learning by doing; the emphasis is on student participation. With the exception of Chapter 9 ('Marley Company Plans to Increase Exports'), where the actual role-playing is by experts and the student participation is vicarious rather than

[1] For a fuller consideration of this issue, see the subsection on 'The Learning Process in Economics' in Chapter 5 below.

direct, all the case studies in this volume rest on a high degree of student participation. One of the contributors, Mrs Sylvia Trench, indicated the value she attached to this feature of case studies when she wrote to the editors that the project in which her students studied a railway closure (Chapter 13) 'seemed to me to be worth an infinite number of lectures on the problems and limitations of cost–benefit analysis'.[1]

Because of the large element of student involvement, the role-playing and project case studies can gain some of the advantage claimed for the Harvard Business School method of opening the way for students to make positive contributions to thought. Independent constructive thinking by students is achieved because they are provided with materials which make it possible for them to think purposefully (see especially the case studies of Chapters 11, 12, 13 and 17) and because the manner of the studies opens up free channels of communication between students and students and between students and teachers.[2] This freedom can lead to a new appreciation of the implications of economic principles, to a new realisation of their applicability and, indeed, to a healthy questioning, and subsequent fuller understanding, of the basis of received theory.

Again, as briefly touched on earlier in considering the use of case studies as illustrations in economics, working with the primary economic data of which many case studies consist has beneficial results. The student becomes aware of some of the difficulties of obtaining the raw material of economics and the assumptions which have to be made in seeking to employ it (see, for example, Chapters 12 and 13); he gains some appreciation of the limitations of survey methods and becomes more critical of the 'findings' of surveys (especially Chapters 14 and 15); he realises the limitations of statistics, including 'official' statistics (as in Chapter 17). In using the data he gains some facility in employing statistical techniques and in presenting statistical results – which can be either at an elementary or an advanced level. The *use* of primary material is a contact with

[1] In the same letter, Mrs Trench also makes the observation, of interest to teachers in universities and colleges, if not to schoolteachers, that this kind of project work with students is not only an excellent teaching instrument but also a very good way of doing research in a manner which avoids the potential conflict between teaching and research.

[2] A. S. Dewing, 'An Introduction to the Use of Cases', in McNair (ed.), *The Case Method at the Harvard Business School.*

reality which helps to create an awareness of the economic structure and an appreciation of the magnitudes of some of the main economic variables in a way which merely reading about them would not do. There is a new dynamic in the learning process.

This dynamic is particularly evident when the student is role-playing; new emotions can be brought to the aid of the learning process. In the role-playing exercise of oligopoly pricing (Chapter 7), the students *feel* the pressure to collude, they do not merely intellectually recognise its existence. Similarly, playing the role of an investor on the Stock Exchange (Chapter 16) draws on a primeval gambling and money-making instinct, which, whatever its morality, arouses the enthusiasm of students to see what capital gains they can succeed in making – even though the gains are imaginary.

Besides these positive merits of the case study in economics, there is a further particular area where the use of case studies may prove of value. Recent years have seen the growth of problem-oriented, interdisciplinary courses, with economics as one of their components. For example, economics may be one of several disciplines forming the foundation of a business studies or of a regional studies course. Likewise many sixth-form economics students also study one or more of economic history, geography, business studies or sociology. Case studies can be used to explore the dividing line between disciplines or to contrast, say, the approach of the economist or the sociologist to a common problem. (Examples in this volume of such interdisciplinary studies are the office location case of Chapter 11 and the field studies outlined in Chapter 15.)

There is also a largely undeveloped potential especially in these interdisciplinary studies, but to some extent also in economics, for the use of case studies as a method of assessment. Not all case studies could serve this purpose, but the use of carefully selected case studies as *part* of the process of assessing students deserves more exploration than it has yet had.

The Limitations and Dangers of Case Studies

If the use of case studies in economics has very real merits, it also carries dangers of which the student, and more especially the teacher, must beware. The student can and should draw on case studies as *part* of that real experience from which he may derive generalisations and give meaning to the abstractions of theory; but there is a danger that he may be led to generalise from an inadequate sample – from too few cases or cases that are unrepresentative. Because the case-study procedure consists of examining some situations in a degree of detail, and because as a teaching method it tends to be more time-consuming than traditional forms of instruction, the more case studies included in any particular course the less the syllabus coverage is likely to be; thus realism in depth may be purchased at the price of realism in breadth. Moreover, two particular difficulties may distort the representative nature of the material used. There may be bias because of the nature of the material; some topics lend themselves to case-study treatment more than others. Or there may be bias because some case material is easier to come by than other material; a firm which has pursued a successful export policy, for example, is more ready to reveal its decisions and its record than one whose export performance is a matter of shame rather than pride.

Especially in role-playing, there is a further danger arising from the choice of material to be included. In this selection, much of course depends on the level of the student. But although a case study necessarily involves a detailed consideration, there is still a problem of *how much* detail – of what to include and what to omit. The teacher has to sail the narrow channel between the Scylla of submerging students in detail and the Charybdis of so simplifying the case that realism, the prime advantage of case studies, is lost.

In economics case studies the object is not usually, as in business case studies, to develop powers of decision-making, but it is worth pointing out the difference between decision-making in case studies and in reality; it is the difference between decision-making with and without responsibility. The latter can never wholly simulate the former. 'Taking decisions' in the intellectual atmosphere of a classroom is a valuable exercise, but it is different from taking decisions under the ruthless pressure of events in business or in politics. Students must at least be made to realise this difference. Role-playing students leave their mistakes behind them in the classroom; they do not have to go on living with the consequences. This itself affects

12

the decision; it is easier to be bold when the penalties of failure are nil or negligible.

Again, almost the worst kind of teaching is the *bad* case study; it demonstrates little but the incompetence of the teacher. Case studies may be bad in a variety of ways. They may be badly chosen or badly implemented. Where possible, subjects should be chosen which appeal to the interest and experience of the group of students concerned – for example, a study of a housing market for twenty-year-olds or the philatelic market for sixteen-year-olds. The teacher must have the necessary competence to carry out the studies; as already indicated in the Introduction, this consideration applies especially to surveys, which form a part of most projects. Surveys and field studies need to be theory-oriented or they become mere fact-finding exercises. The questions to be answered must be clarified and the scope of a project or field study limited, if it is to be effective – indeed, if it is to be a genuine case study. Again, unless responsibilities are clearly defined and allocated to all students in a group, the claim that a case study leads to a high level of student participation will be empty: a project or field study *can* become a tedious bore, or the opportunity for the lethargic student to cultivate idleness.

All this means that the case-study method in economics is no teaching panacea. It requires more work by the teacher, not less, than the traditional methods. If the potential rewards of a good case study are high, the penalties of failure are likewise high. Case studies in economics are one weapon in the armoury of the teacher to be used along with others; and only if used with discretion and a full appreciation of the limitations will the benefits be reaped and the dangers avoided.

Apart from the rather haphazard use of cases as illustrations, so little experiment has been undertaken with case studies in economics that any definitive assessment of their value in economics teaching is impossible. A wide area lies open for research, first to develop suitable case-study material and then to examine and test the relative effectiveness of the traditional teaching as against less of the traditional teaching supplemented by case studies. Let us end simply with two words to encourage teachers to develop and use case-study material. First, the very process of preparing and studying cases for class work is an effective way by which the teacher himself can learn.

13

As Vanderblue and Cragg put it: 'If the teacher is directly concerned with the securing of original case material . . . his opportunities for learning first-hand facts are obvious enough. And in any event the inductive analysis needed in preparing to discuss each case must serve to stimulate new thinking on old problems, and the recognition of implications which might otherwise go wholly unperceived.'[1] The authors/editors endorse the truth of the quotation from their own experiences in preparing this book and its companion volumes. Second, while it has yet to be demonstrated by rigorous testing that case studies are more efficient than traditional methods in helping students to develop and retain economic understanding, there is no doubt that the contributors to this volume have come to believe in their teaching effectiveness. In their various schools, colleges and universities they continue to use case studies and develop new ones, even though the labour of preparation is markedly more than that of the traditional teaching methods.

[1] 'The Case Method of Teaching Economics', loc. cit.

CHAPTER TWO

Planning a Survey

W. W. Daniel

'We'll do a survey.' The number of times this is said among students, journalists, managers, administrators, pressure groups and scholars increases daily and each day we hear and read of the findings of polls and surveys on radio and television and in newspapers and magazines.

In principle this should be a development to be welcomed. At best it means that people in government, administration, politics, business, communications and scholarship increasingly want to know more facts about the people they are concerned with and are less content with 'hunch', speculation and assumptions. They want to test their ideas against reality. They want to know what the people who make up their market, their electorate, their audience, their readership or their area of study are feeling, thinking and doing. The economist has very properly shared in this development. He has become less content to assume that consumers, taxpayers, industrial workers and company directors always make choices and decisions according to principles of economic rationality, but seeks to find out the whole range of factors that influence their choices, decisions and behaviour and establish the part that price, earnings or profits play among these. The very idea of carrying out social surveys involves a change of attitude from certainty to modest open-mindedness and from the acceptance of implicit assumptions to the testing of explicit propositions. As I show (in the example later in this chapter), actually executing the survey imposes an enormous discipline. It becomes no longer enough to talk in vague generalities. You have to spell out exactly what you mean when you put forward a particular idea, proposition or theory. You have to define more exactly its different parts in ways that can be measured. And you have to re-examine critically and refine accepted truths in the light of new evidence.

In principle, then, the advent and popularity of the social survey replaces speculation with fact, arrogance with modesty, and vague generality with precise proposition in at least some aspects of social, political and economic affairs. In practice, however, I am less happy about the spread of social surveying. This year the results of a national survey are published claiming to show that parents do not want compulsory religious education in the Christian faith in schools. Last year one appeared that concluded that they did. A survey of industrial workers reports that the large majority say they would never consider strike action. A few weeks later they are out on strike. One poll demonstrates that people feel that the level of income tax they pay reduces their incentive to work. Another demonstrates that only a tiny minority have an accurate idea of what they actually pay in income tax, which makes it a little difficult for the *actual* level if not the imagined level to influence their behaviour. Polls and surveys have become an instrument of political lobbying and also part of the entertainment business in the media, as well as being used for their proper purposes.

It is small wonder if their findings begin to leave many people confused, bemused or cynical, saying 'Surveys prove nothing', or 'You can prove anything with a survey'. People in authority embrace survey findings enthusiastically when they support their case but talk about 'lies, damned lies, and statistics' when they do not.

What it really means is that people who use, and write about, surveys are all too often totally ignorant of the tool they are using. They are dealing with a foreign language but they do not even understand the vocabulary of the language let alone the grammar and the syntax. A survey of the general population based on asking four ambiguous or meaningless questions of the first 500 people the interviewers meet is given equal weight to one based on a true random sample of 5000 drawn from the electoral roll asking questions that have been extensively tested and validated.

My object in this chapter is to try and outline some of the issues that are relevant to the use of social surveys in economic research, in the hope that this will encourage the reader both to be more critical of the surveys he reads about and to turn to one of the excellent books on survey design if he proposes to employ survey research himself.[1]

Perhaps the best way of going about this would be to start

[1] See also Chapters 3 and 4 below.

with a particular example of an economic issue and the part survey research could play in resolving it.

Let us take the problem of whether the present level of income tax in the United Kingdom reduces the incentive to work among the working population. While this is becoming an issue of increasing public concern and while politicians and economic commentators wax eloquent and confident about the way that 'the crippling level of direct taxation saps incentive among the people who create the nation's wealth', neither economic theory nor our present state of knowledge allows us to say confidently whether it does or not. In economic theory an increase in income tax might reduce incentive or alternatively it might increase incentive. Given that at least part of the reason people work is for money, it might be reasonable to expect that the more of that money you take away in taxation the less they are willing to work – a disincentive effect. Alternatively, on the same basis, it is equally reasonable to expect that the more money you take away in taxation the more people have to work in order to make up for lost income – an incentive effect.

So theory does not get us very far except to point out that the issue is a little more complex than we are sometimes led to believe. So let us try to find out what happens in practice by designing a systematic inquiry.

The first thing we might think of doing is going around asking people how the level of taxation influences their own and other people's behaviour. We could ask employees how it affects their behaviour. We could ask employers how it influences their employees' behaviour. And some investigators have done this. But unfortunately their results are not worth the paper they are printed upon as measures of the way income tax influences working *behaviour*, although they may confirm what we already suspected about *attitudes* towards income tax.

The problem is that a lot of people do not like income tax. They do not like paying it and the more they pay the less they like it. Many of them feel quite strongly about it. They may feel so strongly that they are prepared to attribute every evil that man, industry and the economy is heir to, including the British climate, to the 'crushing level of taxation'.

So income tax is an emotive issue that rouses strong feelings. Some people hate it. Other people quite favour it. If we go around asking them direct questions about how it affects their behaviour, then we can expect their judgement and their answers to be influenced by their feelings. So if we find that a survey has shown that 75 per cent of the population feel that income tax acts as a disincentive, all this may mean is that 75 per cent of the population are not very fond of income tax – an interesting if unsurprising attitudinal finding which does not get us very much further with our problem about how tax influences behaviour.

If we are to get a better idea about how income tax influences behaviour from a survey we must therefore do it indirectly, in a way that conceals from informants the fact that we are interested in income tax, so that their answer will not be influenced by their personal or political feelings about income tax.

So we have to face the question again, how to find out with a survey how income tax influences behaviour. When it becomes a matter of doing something more than just asking people general, direct questions about the effects of tax, we immediately come up against the problem: what behaviour? And this problem indicates one of the main values of carrying out a survey. It is no longer enough to talk in vague generalities about 'the incentive to work' or 'sapping the morale of the creators of the nation's wealth'; it becomes necessary to spell out exactly what aspects of whose working behaviour is felt to be influenced in what directions. If we turn to the arguments of the most committed advocates of the disincentive effect we may not get much help on this. They are content to rely on the 'common-sense' appeal of the view that taking away people's money must reduce their incentive to work, together with the general unpopularity of the tax. But we can help them out by spelling out the different aspects of people's working lives that might be influenced.

1. *Working* v. *non-working*. The first possibility is that a certain level of taxation may discourage some people from taking a job at all. This, of course, could be true only of people who are in a position to work but choose not to; for example:

    (*a*) people who have reached the age of retirement but still have marketable skills, experience and abilities;

    (*b*) certain married women whose family responsibilities do not tie them to the house;

    (*c*) conceivably, some people among the registered unemployed.

2. *Overtime*. People in a position to work overtime may be discouraged from doing so.

3. *Motivation and effort*. The amount of effort that people put into their jobs may be reduced, particularly where they are remunerated by some 'payment by results scheme'.

4. *Second jobs and consultancy*. Wage- and salary-earners who are in a position to take a second part-time job, in the evenings or at weekends, may be discouraged from doing so. Similarly professional people who are offered fee-paying consultancies outside their main employment may decline them.

5. *Promotion and special responsibilities*. People may be reluctant to seek or accept promotion to positions of special responsibility because income tax reduces the value of differential payments.

6. *Employee mobility*. Similarly people may be inhibited from seeking and accepting jobs in other firms or other parts of the country.

7. *Emigration*. Valuable members of the community may be encouraged to emigrate to a country with a tax system they consider more favourable to them.

8. *Absenteeism*. People may be inclined to take occasional time or days off because the financial loss involved is reduced by the tax they would have to pay.

9. *Insecurity among managers*. Some critics of income tax have even suggested that it makes managers and businessmen insecure, conservative and unprepared to take risks because they are unable to amass the type of personal fortune that would make them potentially independent of employers and therefore prepared to question and challenge their superiors.

While these propositions have been expressed in their dis-incentive form, it is equally possible, in all cases other than (7) and (9), to express them in an incentive form. Married women and retired people may find it necessary to return to work because the level of tax reduces other household sources of income, workers may seek overtime and work harder to recover moneys taken in income tax, people may seek second jobs, consultancy and promotion for the same reason, and so on.

Thus the idea of carrying out a survey has already got us a

19

lot further than the original argument by forcing us to spell out the different aspects of different people's working behaviour that might be influenced in different ways.

It does leave us with rather an enormous survey problem, however, if we are to conceive of a single survey that would measure the effects of different levels of taxation in each of these aspects of behaviour and come out at the end with a conclusion on the final balance of effects.

It is probably more realistic to think in terms of doing separate inquiries on each different aspect. For illustrative purposes, let us look at the problem of measuring the effects of the current level of income tax on overtime working.

Again, it is of little value to think of going round asking people whether they ever refuse to work overtime because of the tax they pay on overtime earnings. Apart from the possibility that feelings about income tax will influence answers, this type of questioning invites a certain answer by suggesting it to the informant, and moreover we do not even know if he has the opportunity to work paid overtime at his own option or even if he knows how much tax he would pay on any overtime earnings.

In fact in order to avoid these types of error, it is better to think in terms of a survey of overtime working and the factors that encourage or discourage it, and then see what part income tax plays among these rather than thinking of a survey of the effects of taxation on overtime working.

Such a survey would involve the following stages. The first task is to set out the various possibilities about the different factors that may influence overtime working. We can do this in several ways: by looking at other people's research and ideas on overtime working, by talking informally to workers individually or in groups about overtime working in 'free interviews',[1] and

[1] By 'free interview' we mean giving people an opportunity to talk freely about the topic we are interested in, rather than answering a set of specific questions that we have designed in advance. This allows them to talk about the aspects of the issue that are of interest or importance to them, in a way that they usually talk about them. It shows us the range and types of factor that are important. One very useful way of doing this is, for a group of eight to ten people of the type you are interested in, to discuss the topic among themselves as they would normally with a group of friends over a drink. In this type of 'group discussion' the 'interviewer' plays as small a part as possible, allowing the issues and topics to emerge naturally and spontaneously.

by thinking the problem through. This procedure would show, for instance, that many workers never have any choice about working overtime, and that those who have some control over their own overtime working are influenced by a wide variety of factors in the amount they choose to do, the level of their current H.P. commitments, the nearness of holidays or Christmas, the different sources of income in the household and the pressure from their workmates, for example.

We might also find that there were heated discussions and much confusion about what people actually paid in tax out of their overtime earnings, and that different ideas interacted with other variations via complex ways to determine people's actual overtime working.

On the basis of this preliminary work we can rough out the type of information we need to collect if we are to design a survey to measure systematically the proportions of workers who fall into the different categories we have discovered and the importance of the different factors in influencing the different types of worker. The types of information needed would include:

whether they ever worked paid overtime;
whether they had to work overtime on demand or had any choice over the amount of overtime worked;
how much overtime they worked last week; whether this was more or less than normal;
whether the amount of overtime they chose to work varied from time to time and under what circumstances they were inclined to work more and when less;
whether they ever refused the opportunity of paid overtime; if so, how often and why; if not, why not;
what proportion of their overtime earnings they thought was deducted in tax;
how much they actually paid in tax.

In addition to this we would need to know data about marital status, family composition, household income, H.P. commitments, rent or mortgage payments, standard length of working week, type of shift worked, length of journey to work and method of travel, and full details of the nature of their work and work history.

Having roughed out this information, a draft questionnaire

would be developed to be tested on a small group of workers to see that they understood the questions and that the questions provided meaningful answers. Following this 'pilot' survey the questionnaire is revised accordingly, and if it is satisfactory the survey proper can be carried out.

We then have to decide what population we are interested in surveying and how we are going to sample it. We might be interested in doing this exercise on one particular group of workers in one particular unit of employment. This would have the advantage of allowing us to specify exactly different aspects of the work situation and contracts of employment, and we might be able to supplement our survey data with salary and tax records. Moreover, we could pick a locale that was particularly suited to the issues we wanted to test, that is, one that provided opportunities for almost unlimited discretionary overtime such as some sections of the construction industry. The problem with this would be that we would not know how typical this group of workers was of the working population in general. The alternative procedure of surveying the general working population would give us the broad picture but might not give us sufficient detail for us to carry out the analysis in the depth that we required.

Ideally then we might begin to think in terms of specific local studies done in depth backed up by a national survey to put the 'case studies' into perspective.

But whichever 'populations' we decided to survey, this would still leave us with the problem of how to select our sample. Different types of sample are discussed a little later. Leaving that aside for now, if we collected all the information from a systematic sample of workers, we would then be in a position to carry out two types of analysis.

First, we could analyse informants' own accounts and explanations of their overtime working choices and behaviour. For instance, we could see what proportion ever had the opportunity to work paid overtime at their own option, what proportion ever refused the chance to work paid overtime, what reasons they gave for refusing and how common income tax was among those reasons, and the proportion of those mentioning income tax who actually knew how much they were paying. Secondly, we could analyse the objective data on overtime working; how the number of hours of overtime worked, and frequency of refusal, varied with H.P. commitments, family composition, length of standard working week, level of tax paid and all the other factors listed.

These two types of analysis would enable us to draw confident conclusions about the effect of income-tax payments on overtime working.

This process also illustrates the different stages of survey research, from defining the problem through designing the survey to analysis. It has not been possible to say nearly enough about any of the stages. Volumes could and have been written about interviewing and drafting questions for questionnaires alone. All I can do here is to encourage you to turn to those volumes.[1] The one issue which I would like to comment on in a little more detail, because it is so critical to survey research, is sampling.

SAMPLING

No matter how good your survey and questionnaire design are, no matter how good your interviews and interviewing are, a social survey is a statistical instrument and the value and validity of your findings will be dependent on how representative the people you interview are of the group of people that you are interested in, i.e. how representative your sample is of your target population. This raises the problem of sampling – how to select the people to interview and how many of them to interview.

The only type of sample that permits you to draw conclusions with a known level of mathematical confidence is a true random or probability sample.

What do we mean by a random sample? Producers of magazine programmes on the radio are always doing interviews with people 'selected at random in the street'. What do they actually do? They send a radio interviewer out into the High Street at, say, 10.30 on a Tuesday morning. He stops people and talks to them. If he does this, then his sample will be anything but random. First, the section of the population that is in the High Street of a particular town at 10.30 a.m. on a Tuesday morning is a highly selective group. There will be many non-working housewives there, some office workers and perhaps some visitors.

[1] See Further Reading, p. 29 below, and Chapters 3 and 4 of this volume.

There will not, for instance, be many industrial workers, very few people from other parts of the country, no old-age pensioners confined to the home, and so on.

Secondly, of the people who are there the interviewer's selection will not be random, however much he thinks it is. Some people look friendly, others hostile; some look interesting, others look dull; some are handsome, others are ugly; some look in a desperate hurry, others appear to have all the time in the world; some are alone, others are in pairs or groups; some brush his approaches aside impatiently, others hang around hoping to be approached; and still others say 'Ooh, is it for "Candid Camera"?' and either collapse into giggles or stutter 'I can't think of a thing to say'.

Consciously or unconsciously the interviewer selects them according to his perception of how interesting, approachable and accessible they are. So our so-called 'random' sample ends up as a selected section of a very selective group.

We can avoid part of this problem if we devise what is known as a quota sample. In terms of the general population, for instance, we know a great deal about its general demographic composition. We know what proportion of people fit into each age, sex and occupational group. We know about marital status, family composition and working and non-working housewives. We know what proportions live in different regions.

So we can ensure that the sample we interview is in one sense broadly representative of the general population by setting quota controls for age, sex, occupational group, region and so on, thereby ensuring that the composition of the sample we interview corresponds to the composition of the general population on at least these general criteria.

But this procedure is still far short of perfection. Although we can control these broad general parameters, there may be other characteristics very relevant to the issue we are interested in that we miss out. For instance, we still have the problem that within each quota group the interviewer will consciously or unconsciously select people according to their perceived approachability. Many people approached will refuse and the interviewer will not press them because they are replaceable as long as the replacement fits the quota. If the interviewer approaches people in the street, those in the street during the

24

period when interviewing is carried out may be very different from those who are not, even though they fit the quota; for example, if we are thinking of housewives, women *not* in the street may be those who have their shopping delivered, buy in bulk once a week or fortnight, or are working, characteristics very relevant to many types of consumer choice and spending. If interviews are carried out in homes we know that interviewers will go to areas where they find it most easy to fill quotas, i.e. to council estates for working-class people and to new private housing estates for young middle-class people, thereby missing out the members of each group who live in mixed housing communities. All these sources of bias, and many others you may think of, may distort the sample in significant ways. Moreover, and most importantly, we have no statistical way of measuring or taking account of these distortions and biases. For instance, we cannot measure sampling error in a quota sample although as we shall see later we can do in a true random sample.

Nevertheless, we know from experience that a good quota sample, controlling for the main demographic characteristics together with any others that are obviously relevant to the survey subject (e.g. doing a consumer survey in convenience foods we should obviously have to control for working and non-working housewives), will give us a good general guide to attitudes, opinions and preferences, as long as we do not want or need to be exact to between 5 and 10 per cent.

On the other hand, if we want exact information on behaviour, ownership or intentions, and we need to know exactly the limits of our data, then we have no alternative to a true random, probability sample.

A true random sample is one in which every member of the target population has an equal chance of being selected and thus those actually selected are chosen by chance. We have already seen that our other methods of sampling do not give everyone an equal chance of selection. Those who live in certain areas or certain types of housing, those who have certain behaviour patterns or certain types of appearance, have more chance of being selected than others. In a random sample we have a list of the total population we are interested in. We select a sample from this list on a random basis and we have a list of pre-selected informants to interview. We try to interview all of them and record those who cannot be contacted or refuse to be interviewed. From our knowledge of the size of the population, the sample size and the success rate we can calculate the sampling error with statistical exactness.

For instance, if we are thinking of measuring voting intentions on a national basis, we select electoral units on a random basis. Then we get the electoral register for each of the electoral units selected, and select names from the list using a set of random numbers. We issue the names and addresses to interviewers who carry out interviews and record unsuccessful contacts. From this we may find, for instance, that 45 per cent of the people we interviewed intend to vote Labour. This means, given a sampling error of, say, 2·5 per cent, that we can conclude with statistical confidence that between 42·5 per cent and 47·5 per cent of the population will vote Labour.

From this it is clear that in theory there is no real alternative to a random sample for a social survey. In practice the only disadvantage is that it is more difficult and complicated to administer and execute, and in real financial terms can cost up to four times as much as a quota sample for the same number of informants. It is not surprising therefore if quota samples are so popular; and as we have seen, they can be adequate for certain purposes as long as we are aware of their limitations. It does mean though, that however boring it may seem compared to all the exciting findings revealed by a survey, the first question you have to ask is, what was the method of sampling used and what level of statistical confidence can be placed on the findings? It is amazing how few people ask this question and what completely meaningless conclusions they draw as a result.

The basic point here is, again, that the survey is a statistical tool and as such it is concerned with establishing proportions and relationships, *within certain levels of probability*. Thus, survey findings never 'prove' anything in the logical sense of the word. What they do is produce findings that are acceptable or not to certain levels of confidence. So when we are evaluating our findings, what we are chiefly concerned about is establishing whether the variations and proportions that emerge are such as might occur by chance or, alternatively, are so unlikely to have occurred by chance that we can accept them as indicative of real variations.

For instance, if in our survey of overtime we found that 40

per cent of those with non-working wives sometimes refused the opportunity to work overtime, whereas 55 per cent of those with working wives did, this would suggest that whether or not his wife was earning influenced a worker's propensity to accept opportunities for working overtime. But there is the possibility, depending on the size of our sample in relation to the total population (the total number of people in the group we are sampling), that this variation might have occurred by chance rather than representing a real difference. Thus we subject the finding to a test of statistical significance. We calculate the proportions that we would expect to find in each category if there were *no* difference between willingness to work overtime among those with and without working wives respectively, and we incorporate these into a mathematical formula together with the figures we actually found. The result enables us to establish how likely our figures are to have occurred by chance. We may find, for instance, that it is 100 to 1 against our figure having occurred by chance and we can conclude that the relationship between willingness to work overtime and not having a working wife is established at the ·01 level of significance.

Once again this is not the place to go into detail about the different types of significance tests that are used, nor the mathematics behind them. The purpose here is to illustrate how we approach survey findings and encourage you to turn to the references at the end of the chapter for more detail.

In conclusion, a warning should be added about the use of social surveys for testing economic theory. This is that any survey on the factors that influence the behaviour of consumers, taxpayers, employees or businessmen is likely to appear to cast doubt on economic theory without necessarily doing so.

Let us take, for example, economic theory of labour mobility in local labour markets. According to classical economic theory such mobility is determined by relative wage rates, *all other things being equal*. Given similar types of work and similar conditions of employment, workers will be attracted towards those employers paying higher wage rates and away from those paying lower ones, and relative wage changes are assumed to be the best way of encouraging a balanced distribution of labour.

If we carry out surveys of industrial workers, however, asking them why they take jobs, why they change jobs, why they do

27

not change jobs and how they look for jobs, we find a pattern of answers that appears to cast doubt on this theory. Wages do not feature very high in responses compared to other aspects of the work and its context. Choices are often made in complete ignorance of the relative characteristics of different jobs. A very high value is placed on security by many industrial workers so that they are reluctant to consider job changes even though they could get higher rewards elsewhere. In fact job-changing behaviour seems to be governed more by habit and ignorance than knowledge and rational choice on the economic model, and where choices are made these tend often to be made on grounds other than financial ones.

In the face of this type of evidence it is tempting to reject classical economic theory. But this omits the possibility that nevertheless relative wage levels play a sufficiently significant part, for a sufficiently significant proportion of workers, to make the economic model useful in practice although the economic model of choice is not valid for all or even a majority of individual industrial workers.

The analogy that always occurs to me in this context is that of the postal questionnaire, which is particularly appropriate to this chapter. If you send out a short questionnaire by post to people and ask them to return it completed, you can expect about 50 per cent to do so. If, however, you include the offer of a small payment for a completed questionnaire the response may rise to 65 per cent. The significantly higher success rate when using a financial reward is inclined to elicit the comment that this shows how people are motivated by money. In fact it does the opposite. It shows that only 15 per cent of people are motivated by money in this context. 50 per cent would have responded anyway. And a further 35 per cent still did not respond despite the financial incentive.

But the 'economic theorist' who works on the basis that people are interested in financial reward in this context would have better results in practice even though his 'theory of human behaviour' was invalid in general, in so far as it did not apply to 85 per cent of the population. The 'psychologist' who took the view that financial rewards were of marginal importance, appealing only to a small minority, would be right, but would have a much poorer survey to show as a result if he based his practice on his theory.

FURTHER READING

The following books cover in greater detail the different aspects of survey research indicated in the chapter:

Social science research methods in general:

P. H. Mann, *Methods of Sociological Enquiry* (Oxford, 1968).

Social survey design, execution and analysis:

C. A. Moser, *Survey Methods in Sociological Investigation* (London, 1958).
A. Hancock, *Survey* (London, 1964).

Statistical tools for social scientists:

T. C. Connolly and W. Sluckin, *An Introduction to Statistics for the Social Sciences* (London, 1962).

CHAPTER THREE

Drafting a Questionnaire

Michael Rose

INTRODUCTION

The present chapter attempts to offer some guidance on those aspects of questionnaire design – the form and phrasing of specific inquiries – which usually cause the social surveyor the greatest amount of purely *technical* trouble at this stage of a project. But it should be recognised at the outset that in a most important sense the *methodological* problem of *which* questions should be asked is a prior and more crucial one than that of *how* to ask them.

Unfortunately it is wellnigh impossible to provide advice about what particular questions should be asked without a good deal of information about the precise research aims of a given survey. Considerable uncertainty usually arises here for the inexperienced surveyor, however, precisely because he is himself unsure exactly what his research aims are. The first step in drafting a questionnaire, then, is to specify in as precise detail as possible what new information the research is trying to discover. The researcher must demand of himself, insistently and continually: What is my *problem*?

His problem is likely to be one of two main sorts. Either, firstly, he simply wishes to fill a gap in his information about the distribution of certain characteristics among members of a certain population; or, secondly, he wishes to test some hypothesis about the relationship between two or more variable properties which occur in members of a population. ('Population' is used here in its statistical sense.) In the first instance his general aim may be described as *descriptive*; in the second, as *explanatory*. The reader must be referred to the literature for an adequate discussion of the implications of these varying objectives.[1] But we may note that the formulation of a survey with

[1] Herbert Hyman, *Survey Design and Analysis* (New York, 1955) chap. 2.

explanatory purposes will usually complicate appreciably the problems of choosing what to ask. One reason is that the researcher will be hoping to demonstrate relationships, ideally of a causal kind, between variables. To do so successfully will involve him in showing that other variables which are potentially causal of some phenomenon do not in fact exert an influence. He must therefore collect data about such variables. Yet, beforehand, he may be most uncertain about which variables are indeed of this type.

One method of approaching this problem of what to ask is to devise mock statistical tabulations which, if they contained figures, would show the distribution of some variable property in a population, or how possession of it is related to the possession of another or several other personal attributes. In effect the researcher asks himself 'What tabulations shall I need to write an adequate report of my findings?'

Suppose, for instance, his general problem is to determine the extent of utilisation of bus services in a certain town. At the very least he will require a simple statistical table which indicates the proportions of his sample which made, or did not make, at least one journey by bus in, say, a given week. Such a table is certainly a start, but will convey only rudimentary information: x per cent, it will tell us, made a journey, while y per cent did not. Already the surveyor can visualise a more helpful table: one which would, for example, divide the respondents into those who made no journeys at all, and those who made between one and five journeys, between six and ten, and above ten.

The surveyor might then consider the possibility of defining more carefully the persons who fall into each of these degrees of bus utilisation. Who, for example, are the 'heavy users' who made more than ten journeys in the week? Perhaps they are the very young or the retired. If so, he will need a suitable table relating usage to age: hence he must ask respondents their ages. Perhaps they are housewives. Or simply people who do not own cars. By asking appropriate questions he will be able to describe 'heavy users' in greater detail, compare them with 'non-users', and to some extent assess the association of certain attributes, or clusters of attributes, with varying levels of bus utilisation.

This anticipation of results may seem an obvious procedure,

and indeed all surveyors adopt it in some form or another. Usually, however, it is an operation carried out entirely 'in the head'. Unfortunately, this often results in the surveyor forgetting the 'mental notes' he has made to ask for information which would generate the additional tables he has suddenly visualised. If mock tables are in fact drawn, or noted down, this is less likely to happen. To continue the above example, it might occur to us as we draw up our tables that we could also make good use of one which indicated how far respondents lived from their place of work, school, etc. If we immediately add it to our list it will not slip our mind.

A further advantage of this process of anticipating relations between findings, which cannot be elaborated here, is that it will guide us in deciding the required size of the sample.

TYPES OF QUESTIONNAIRE

It is useful to distinguish four main types of questionnaire, and it is probable that the reader has had some experience of each of them at some time as a respondent in someone else's survey.

The Interview Guide

This is a rather loosely structured questionnaire instrument, probably little more than an *aide-memoire* to the interviewer in some cases, consisting of a set of topics to be covered with the respondent. The interviewer is therefore given great discretion in phrasing his inquiries and determining the order in which they are put. Its great virtue, then, is flexibility. This flexibility may enable the interview to approximate more closely than is possible with other types of questionnaire to the rhythms of a 'natural' conversation. For some survey purposes, for example exploratory interviews with specialists who can provide helpful background information about a problem which will later be studied more rigorously, it is most useful.

However, it should be evident that firstly it should only be administered by the more experienced interviewer who is fully conversant with the purposes of the research. Secondly, and possibly less evidently, it tends to produce results which from a strict methodological viewpoint can only be judged as unreliable. This is because its flexibility may produce uncontrolled errors of response; in other words, the surveyor will usually be unable to assess to what extent the replies were influenced by differences in the wording of a question used by the interviewer with different respondents, and variation of the order of inquiries.

The Interview Schedule

In contrast to the *interview guide*, the *interview schedule* is a highly structured form of instrument. It contains a finalised set of questions in a carefully determined sequence. The wording of each inquiry has been established by discussion among the research team and tested experimentally in the field on a small group of respondents similar to those to whom the questionnaire will finally be administered. This pre-test should have established those formulations of an inquiry which cause misunderstanding on the part of the respondent, or biased or ambiguous replies. When he administers it in the field the interviewer should never depart from the standardised wording and order of questions. Nor should he introduce additional or supplementary questions except under carefully prescribed conditions.[1] The hope is that the high level of standardisation of this type of questionnaire will at least help to hold constant – though it cannot ever fully remove – any biasing factors in the form of inquiries.

Mail Questionnaires

Questionnaires which are sent to respondents through the post must generally be very highly structured indeed. If a respondent does misunderstand an inquiry on an *interview schedule*, the interviewer is usually able to repeat it in such a way as to make it intelligible. In the last resort he could rephrase it or explain exactly what information is being requested. Since the *mail questionnaire* is completed by the respondent himself, its inquiries must rigorously exclude all vagueness and ambiguity. They should also be of a simple, factual variety, and permit rapid and simple recording of replies. Again, since no interviewer is present to generate the personal 'rapport' which may motivate a respondent to complete a long interview, the mail questionnaire should be short. It should also be remembered that

[1] See 'Probing', Chapter 4, p. 51 below.

33

although the use of mail questionnaires considerably lowers the cost of an inquiry, it may lead to rather unreliable results: respondents may discuss the questionnaire with someone else before 'hitting on good answers', or even give it to a friend to complete; furthermore a very large proportion of schedules are not returned at all.[1]

Supervised Self-Administered Questionnaires

This final type is an occasionally used compromise between the cheapness of the mail questionnaire and the advantages of having present a member of the research team when the schedule is completed. The procedure is to distribute schedules to a number of respondents concentrated in one place, for example to a class of students. The respondent fills out the questionnaire himself, preferably on the spot, and the researcher is available to answer queries and ensure completion by all, or almost all, of the respondents. An additional advantage from a methodological point of view is that the variable of *time* is virtually held constant. Thus the researcher may be able to claim that certain types of opinion did not differ between two respondents simply because certain developments in current affairs occurred between the day the first was interviewed and the later day when the second was approached. However, all these advantages are offset by the fact that the need to obtain a relatively centralised group of respondents forces upon the researcher a usually unrepresentative sample.

TYPES OF QUESTION

Whichever type of questionnaire is selected for the particular piece of research being undertaken, the surveyor must decide in what particular form he must cast the inquiries. A broad, but crucial, distinction can be made at this point between 'open-ended' (otherwise 'free-choice') and 'closed' (otherwise 'forced-choice') question forms. These are discussed below.

Open-ended questions are so phrased that the respondent is invited to volunteer a reply in his own terms, the entire response

[1] W. J. Goode and P. K. Hatt, *Methods in Social Research* (New York, 1952) chap. 12.

being recorded verbatim as a general rule. Such an inquiry might be: (1) 'How much do you manage to save from your income?'; or (2) 'Why do people say it is a good thing to encourage children to save money?' In neither of these questions are there any terms or categories suggested which might guide the respondent's replies. In the case of the first, for example, a reply might be in terms of any quantity of pounds or pence for any period of time. Answers such as '£2 a week', '25p a week', or 'There's a hole in my pocket – I never save anything' would all be equally acceptable.

Closed questions, on the other hand, offer the respondent a limited but logically exhaustive set of mutually exclusive possible responses, one of which he is 'forced' to select. Instead of having to record a verbatim answer, all the interviewer has to do is to place a tick beside the appropriate response (all of which are printed on the schedule), or encircle an appropriate code number on the schedule. In mail, or other types of self-administered questionnaire, the respondent will write his own tick or circle. We can easily transform questions 1 and 2 above into a simple closed form:

3. How much do you manage to save from your income; would you say it was on average

    (i) £3 a week or more?
    (ii) At least £1 a week but less than £3?
    (iii) Something, but less than £1 a week?
    (iv) Nothing at all?

4. Why do people say it is a good thing to encourage children to save money? Would you say it was

    (i) Because they believe it will teach children to manage money in general?
    (ii) Because they believe it will teach children self-discipline in general?
    (iii) Because they believe it is good for the country for everyone to save money?
    (iv) For some other reason?

In designing any questionnaire it must be decided which inquiries should be cast in an open-ended and which in a closed form. The manifest advantage of the open-ended question is that it does not impose on the respondent a set of categories which are foreign to his mode of thinking on an issue. On questions which attempt to probe for opinions and attitudes, this freedom tends to increase the realism of the reply, since the respondent is not forced to pick an answer which only approximates to his real feelings. Secondly, open-ended questions stimulate spontaneity: they invite the respondent to talk freely and suggest that the nuances of his own views are important. Thus they may increase the rapport between interviewer and respondent and lead to a general improvement of the quality of all his answers.

Furthermore, the importance of the issue to the respondent can often be inferred from the nature of his reply to an open-ended question. For example, in answer to question 1 above, one respondent's verbatim reply might run: 'I'm not sure. I've never gone into that. I've got a Post Office book, but it's just the odd bob or two here and there.' A second might reply: 'Only a few shillings now and then. It's awful, isn't it? But however much you worry about the future the money just seems to go.' Now clearly from these verbatim replies we could with some plausibility argue that saving is a much more salient economic value for respondent number two than it is for the more happy-go-lucky respondent number one. Yet if we were to have used the closed form of this question (3 above), both respondents would have been recorded (or 'coded') for identical replies. Therefore it is apparent that open-ended questions can reduce some of the artificiality which the survey inevitably produces in the picture of social reality.

However, there are many offsetting disadvantages of the open-ended question. Firstly, answers to some open-ended questions require a good deal of thought on the part of the respondent and may tax his powers of self-expression. He may therefore say the first thing that comes into his head or deny that he possesses the knowledge or opinion sought. His sense of inadequacy may create resentment of the interviewer, thereby dissipating rapport and co-operativeness. Secondly, open-ended questioning usually demands a relatively high level of interviewer skill and motivation. The interviewer may become tired of having to record long verbatim replies and merely select those sections of them which seem relevant. Thirdly, and most importantly, open-ended questions are heavily time-

36

consuming and may thus add to the total costs in time and money of the survey. Fourthly, and partly associated with the foregoing objection, the analysis of the replies to open-ended questions is often difficult. The technique adopted (content analysis) cannot be described here, but reference to the suggested sources will convince the reader that it requires considerable expertise.[1]

The relative advantages and disadvantages of the closed question are more or less the reverse of those of the open-ended question. In their favour it can be said firstly that reliance on them shortens the length of the average interview (and this makes possible some interviews, like bus-stop polling in transport studies, not otherwise possible) and hence reduces unit costs. Secondly, they help to focus the attention of the respondent on issues, or on aspects of an issue, which are most relevant to the researcher's need for information. For example, what may matter to the researcher is simply that 30 per cent of his sample never save money. That some of the people comprising this proportion feel guilty about their 'improvidence', others proud of it, and others indifferent, may be totally irrelevant for him. Thirdly, they demand less interviewing skill. Fourthly, they simplify the business of analysis: answer categories can be 'pre-coded', that is, allocated code numbers which correspond to those provided on each column of standard punched cards. The chore of transcribing the data from schedules to punched cards prior to machine tabulation is therefore greatly simplified.

For these and other reasons, not the least of which is the apparently more 'scientific' format of a neat set of response categories on the schedule, a quality which has a beguiling appeal to the novice surveyor, closed questions may seem to have the edge on the open-ended forms. Yet the reader can confidently be assured that the closed question often forces the respondent to give rather unrealistic replies, lends the interview an unpleasant air of the 'official interrogation', and may generally distort the whole body of information obtained from him. Interviewers may tire of endlessly listing alternative answers from which the respondent may choose and fill in 'for him' an answer which would seem plausible from his previous replies. Error may creep in also in a purely mechanical way:

[1] L. Festinger and D. Katz, *Research Methods in the Behavioral Sciences* (New York, 1966) chap. 10.

questionnaires full of closed questions often proceed at a brisk pace and the interviewer's pencil may 'slip a notch' and tick a 'yes' when a 'no' has been given.

No final set of decision rules can be offered here for providing the ultimate balance between inquiries in each of these two forms on any questionnaire. However, it is recommended that a schedule should contain inquiries in both forms, sometimes to deal with different aspects of the same issue. One very sensible procedure is to undertake a pilot study in which half of the respondents receive the inquiry in an open-ended form and the other half in a closed form. Answers between the two groups can then be compared, and the form which is apparently the more productive for the purpose in hand adopted. Again, the answers in a pilot study to an initially open-ended inquiry can be analysed to yield a more realistic set of response categories for a final closed form than could have been thought up in the abstract by the research team. The apparent compromise of 'field-coding' is not recommended.[1]

QUESTION ORDER

An important consideration associated to some extent with that of the relative merits of open-ended and closed questions is that of question order. This has two aspects, what might be considered the 'strategic' and the 'tactical'. The strategic issues bear on the problem of where to locate specific inquiries, or a set of related inquiries on a single issue, in the questionnaire as a whole. The tactical issue is that of how to order particular questions which constitute a related set, or 'battery'. A suggestive cliché for dealing with both these forms of the problem is to pursue not what appears to the surveyor the correct logical order, but the correct *psychological* order.[2] Let us attempt to illustrate briefly what this means.

From the strategic point of view, if we place certain questions near the opening of the questionnaire they may create suspicion or hostility which colours all subsequent replies (if any, in some cases). Hence, it would be foolish to begin by asking a

[1] A. N. Oppenheim, *Questionnaire Design and Attitude Measurement* (London, 1966) pp. 44-5.
[2] Ibid., chap. 2.

38

respondent to reveal his income or to offer us a rating of his own social status. Delicate matters such as these should be introduced later in the schedule. (It is apparent, incidentally, that question order is of far less importance with mail questionnaires, since they are usually read through quickly before they are filled out.) As a general rule, then, the first section of a questionnaire should contain relatively simple, emotionally inert questions which encourage the respondent to talk; the second section should deal with more profound factual matters and the touchier emotional issues; the final section can then permit answers which somewhat relieve the emotional tension built up in the previous section and restore any damage caused to the rapport between interviewer and respondent.[1]

Turning to the tactical aspect, it is vital that, with sequences of questions concerned with exploring related aspects of a single major issue, we do not begin with a question which suggests that the respondent *should* have information, experience or opinion which in fact he may lack. Once having been forced to claim knowledge, he may subsequently feel obliged to answer the supplementary questions, feeling that any response is preferable to admitting his ignorance.

Suppose we were asking respondents about their knowledge of, and opinion about, Britain's relationship with the European Common Market. It would be most unwise to begin with an inquiry such as: (5) 'Would Britain gain or lose in economic terms from joining the Common Market?' We could well find that a substantial minority of respondents replied with a confident 'yes' but with a slightly glazed look about the eyes which suggested that they had had insufficient time to decide in their own mind the difference between the Common Market and the Stock Market. Again, suppose we were inquiring about participation in trade union activities. We might wish to know how often trade unionists voted in union elections. But it would be foolish in the extreme to begin the sequence of questions with an inquiry on this aspect of union activity, if only because the respondent might not indeed be a member of a trade union in the first place.

The techniques which help us to order questions successfully in each of these instances are known as *funnelling* and *filtering*. Funnelling, as the term suggests, is the ordering of questions so

[1] J. Galtung, *Theory and Methods of Social Research* (London, 1967).

that we proceed from the very general to the detailed particular. For example, we would preface question 5 above with a general inquiry which introduced the issue of the Common Market and gave us some indication of the respondent's awareness or interest in the issue as a whole. (The form of the inquiry might well be open-ended.) This would give the respondent some chance to reflect, to marshal, and to begin organising any thoughts he has on the issue. We could then proceed with increasingly detailed probing of his knowledge and opinion, if necessary calling a halt at any point where it became apparent that his contribution was exhausted. Filtering is an analogous technique whereby the answer to an initial question determines whether subsequent questions will be asked at all, or if so, which ones. Before asking our respondent how often he votes in union elections, we inquire whether he is a trade union member. These procedures are undoubtedly to a large extent applied common sense, but it is only when we come to the actual task of designing appropriate funnelling and filtering question sequences that we may begin to appreciate the effort required to maintain consistent and workable commonsensicality.

QUESTION PHRASING

Variations in the phrasing of any inquiry are liable to stimulate varying responses, and some formulations may produce no response at all. Let us contrast for one only half-frivolous moment the following inquiries of a latecomer: 'Why are you late?'; 'Why are you *so* late?'; 'What kept you?'; 'What time is this?'; and 'Well?' All formulations seek essentially the same piece of information, yet clearly only one – and if the reader cannot identify it, he should abandon any ambitions as a social surveyor – is likely to elicit a brief, relevantly informative and relatively unbiased response. In the questionnaire, inquiries should be so phrased that their meaning is clear and unambiguous, that they contain no implied emotional threat, and that they do not guide the respondent towards an answer that misrepresents his true feelings or situation. They must, therefore, be purged of the frequently biasing factors in the structure, wording or tone of most 'everyday' inquiries. Yet they should certainly sound *as if* they were indeed 'everyday' inquiries. The surveyor has no resort to some completely neutral 'official' or 'scientific' language. He cannot afford to ape the emasculated equivocation of a Royal Commission report. To inquire 'What is the reason, if any, for the measured discrepancy between your expected and actual times of arrival?' would probably be less productive overall than a terse 'Where the hell have you been?'

This latter point is made because apprentice surveyors especially are liable to cast their inquiries in a rather stilted form. One rule often offered to them therefore is to select only those words and phrases which will be understood by the least educated respondent. Yet if the survey is to cover an educationally wide cross-section of the population, the writer believes it is not a rule to follow slavishly. More educated respondents may become irritated by the feeling that the surveyor is talking down to them, while the occasionally misunderstood word can sometimes be explained. We should bear in mind that nearly everyone's vocabulary of comprehension is rather wider than the range of words they habitually use. But once again, the best solution to this problem is the careful study of the results of a pilot survey.

As a working principle it is advisable, however, to prefer an Anglo-Saxon to a Latin vocabulary. It may be tempting to inquire of redundant workers 'When did the company intimate that you would become redundant?', but 'tell you' would be preferable to 'intimate' ('become redundant', although it employs a 'latinism', is of course a well-understood term, and to substitute some alternative such as 'lose your job' might in this instance be slightly productive of bias). However, if one chooses to steer away from 'long words' towards the more basic forms of English (and some specialists do indeed advocate that the very limited vocabularies of 'Basic English' compiled by linguists should be adhered to), then one must not fall into the opposite trap of trying to utilise the often homely familiarity of slang. To inquire of a sample of motorists if they have ever been 'convicted' of a motoring offence may sound rather formal and vaguely threatening, but it would none the less be preferable to asking whether they had ever 'been done'.

Slang is the private language of a specific group and we cannot predict beforehand that each respondent will be familiar with it. What is true for slang expressions is true for techni-

41

calities. Thus a political pollster should avoid asking, for example, about people's opinion of the 'British electoral principle of the simple majority' in Parliamentary elections; the economic surveyor likewise cannot usually ask people directly about, for example, the value of 'British invisible exports'. If either were to do so they would in many instances simply fail to communicate. The only solution open is often to employ some relatively cumbrous circumlocution or to follow the technicality with illustrations of its meaning. Thus the political pollster might have to refer to 'the method used in this country where the candidate with more votes than any other is the outright winner, even though the votes for other candidates are more than his when they are added together'; and the economic surveyor might have to add the explanation 'by invisible exports we're thinking of things like insurance, shipping and banking services and so on sold to foreigners'.

The foregoing brief remarks, and indeed this chapter as a whole, can be no more than broadly illustrative of some of the general and particular problems of drafting an efficient, purposeful questionnaire which is as free as possible from those factors which produce incomprehension and biased replies. The reader is now urgently advised to consult those references provided already and those which follow. If he does so he will avoid the more disastrous mistakes often made by novices and may produce a questionnaire instrument which leads to valuable and interesting findings.

FURTHER READING

A. N. Oppenheim, *Questionnaire Design and Attitude Measurement* (London, 1966).

W. J. Goode and P. K. Hatt, *Methods in Social Research* (New York, 1952).

C. Selltiz *et al.*, *Research Methods in Social Relations* (London, 1965).

CHAPTER FOUR

Interviewing Technique

Michael Rose

INTRODUCTION

It is often said that the successful social research interview will approximate to the form of that much commoner encounter between two persons, the conversation. What seems largely intended by this suggestion is that if the purely *personal* communication between interviewer and respondent can acquire some of that depth, sensitivity and emotional involvement characteristic of the 'good' conversation, then the quality and precision of the factual data which will be obtained from the respondent is likely to become more extensive and reliable. Undeniably there is much that is plausible in this claim: the development of a certain degree of that mutual involvement and sensitive response conveyed by the notion of 'rapport' is perhaps inseparable from the acquisition of the richer varieties of personal material.

It will presently be argued that there are limitations to this analogy. The reader will probably already have reflected that many – probably the great majority of – everyday conversations, although emotionally pleasurable to both parties, and in that sense communicative, have very little indeed to do with the structured transmission of specific attitudinal or factual data. In a word, then, a social survey interview is not, and must not be allowed to deteriorate into, either a 'natter' or a 'heart to heart'.

Yet one consideration that the conversational analogy correctly reminds us of is that a precondition of good interviewing is an ability in the interviewer to recognise those elements of interpersonal behaviour summed up in the expression 'non-verbal communication'. The reader is strongly recommended to consult some of the recent socio-psychological literature on

43

this subject.[1] All that can be done here is to recall that the social skills of a good conversationalist demand, besides the manipulation of words, the manipulation of bodily appearance and movement, of facial and eye gestures, and of the tone of the voice, to mention only a few broad types of non-verbal behaviour.

And no less important than the ability of the conversationalist to mould his own behaviour in the light of these principles is his ability to recognise the appearance of key 'gestures' and 'cues' in the behaviour of the other party and to interpret correctly their meaning. Such observational and interpretative skills seem to be acquired and to operate intuitively in the lucky few. But the rest of us can take heart from the fact that it is eminently possible to train ourselves in them.

In practical terms, skill in this area will enable the interviewer to learn a great deal about the respondent before a single question is put. Some outline predictions of the respondent's later behaviour can be made and consequently so can contingency plans by the interviewer to adjust his own behaviour. Dress, facial expressions, hand movements, posture – even, or perhaps especially, when they are deliberately controlled to create a desired impression – are all potential 'telltales' and the skilled interviewer should be able to read them accordingly. Yet in saying this, one is most certainly *not* saying that the interviewer should immediately categorise the respondent in terms of some arbitrary theory of social or psychological types. Social reality is more complex than theories which divide people into 'introverts' and 'extroverts', the 'innerdirected' and the 'other-directed', and so on, suggest – or indeed, to be fair to the theorists, intend to suggest.

The interviewer must remember that just as he is trying to read the respondent, so is the respondent, in terms of his own experience, trying to read the interviewer. Clearly, it is vital that his immediate impression, and later observations, should not distort the encounter. How, then, should the interviewer, in general, 'present himself?'.

Here we see the limits of the conversational analogy. When all is said and done, the interviewer approaches the respondent with a declared and explicit purpose: to obtain private infor-

[1] Michael Argyle, *The Psychology of Interpersonal Behaviour* (London, 1967).

44

mation. As with the good conversationalist, true enough, his ability to obtain the necessary information will involve the manipulation of emotional rewards, but he cannot dismiss the essential features of his role as information-gatherer. Nor should he try to.

At first, it might seem that his true function as information-gatherer casts him anyway in a role, that of the prying outsider, which is impossible to support. But this is highly pessimistic. There is a good deal of truth in the claim that survey interviewing is becoming such a widespread activity that it has already developed its own widely known and accepted etiquette. Consequently, in a large number of instances, interviewer and respondent automatically adopt the expected, and accepted, patterns of behaviour associated with the respective roles. While these assertions perhaps hold stronger for the United States than for the United Kingdom, we are undoubtedly moving in the direction of the former. Therefore, the appropriate role for the interviewer to adopt, and to attempt to sustain, is that of . . . interviewer!

Since the occupational role of interviewer is a semi-professional, white-collar one, the interviewer's appearance and manner should be consistent with what is expected of persons who occupy such statuses. His clothes, for example, should be plain, neat and clean. If he is a dedicated follower of fashion he should resolve, in the interests of science, to follow it in his leisure hours. Nor should he imagine that to dress as his respondents do (or as he assumes they do) will necessarily make him more acceptable: if he is detailed to interview a sample of industrial workers he will probably create an unfortunate effect if he arrives at the factory-gates in a clothcap. Respondents, he can be assured, will almost always expect signs of a vaguely professional status. And such signs extend beyond the superficialities of dress.

His speech, for example, should steer between the 'affected' and the folksy. He should convey an impression of unobtrusive efficiency, alertness and confidence. While good humour is probably an essential underlying qualification for interviewing, in view of its occasional stresses, he should also suggest seriousness of intent. Presumably the survey would not have been conducted unless its potential findings were considered important, and it would be an impertinence to respondents, whose

45

time is just as valuable as anyone else's, to give any other impression.

The reader can pursue for himself elsewhere[1] these more general, but most important, theoretical aspects of interviewing as a research method and the interviewer's role. We turn now to a selective list of more practical problems which may occur in the field as the interviewer goes about his work.

MAKING CONTACT WITH THE RESPONDENT

The interviewer's first problem is to make contact with the respondent and obtain his agreement to the interview. If the schedule is brief and to be administered quickly to passers-by in the street, this will usually be achieved readily enough by simply accosting a prospective respondent and announcing, for example: 'Good morning, I am from (e.g. Goole Polytechnic) and we are conducting a survey of local opinion about (e.g. car-parking/unemployment/noise/bus-services). Now could I ask you. . . .' The first question can follow immediately, and so, in nearly all cases, will the first reply.

However, not all surveys are of the very simple kind that can rely on brief street interviews, and for them a more lengthy introduction will usually be necessary. Often a letter is sent to the respondent before an interviewer calls explaining the purposes of the survey, how the respondent was selected, and assuring him of the confidentiality with which his replies will be treated. But even when this very wise precaution has been taken, the interviewer himself will need, in most cases, to repeat such reassurances. Respondents frequently suspect interviewers to be disguised encyclopedia salesmen or other kinds of sophisticated commercial hawker. Alternatively, they develop an uneasy suspicion that the interviewer has been sent by 'them' to 'check up' on him. Quite often they perceive the interview as a sort of quiz and fear they will come out with a poor showing. For all these, and other, reasons they may therefore refuse to be interviewed.

It is crucial that the interviewer prevent suspicion, as refusals reduce the statistical validity of any results. Hence, the interviewer's introduction should include assurances about his true identity (identity cards from the survey director should be

[1] H. H. Hyman *et al.*, *Interviewing in Social Research* (Chicago, 1955).

carried for this purpose), that replies will be treated in confidence, that there are no 'right' or 'wrong' answers to any of the questions, and that everyone's opinions on the issue being studied are valuable. Since people often worry about how they came to be selected for interview, a brief description of the sampling procedure can be given.

These introductory assurances may take the form of a standardised patter to be delivered to all respondents, even to those who express immediate willingness to co-operate (the majority). And this is perhaps the safest practice when relatively inexperienced interviewers are to be employed. But if there is no standardised introduction, then replies to possible objections should be thought out and memorised. These can then be introduced automatically as need dictates. For example:

Respondent: How've you managed to pick on me?

Interviewer: All the names and addresses we have were chosen from the Register of Electors in line with a statistical scheme. Anyone on the Register had an equal chance of being chosen. Your name just happened to come out, just like you could win a raffle.

Respondent: Well, you say this survey's to do with economics and all that, so you'd better speak to my husband. Men have more ideas in that department.

Interviewer: We often find that the people who are more modest about themselves have just as interesting and important things to say as anyone. Besides, we want our survey to cover all groups of people, young and old, men and women. So if we left out the ladies we wouldn't get a proper cross-section, would we?

Whichever practice is chosen, the watchwords are anticipation and preparation. Nothing is worse than for an interviewer to be confronted with one of these initial objections and to have to fumble for an explanation. Suspicions and uncertainties are inevitably multiplied.

One problem which occasionally occurs at the contact-making stage is to ascertain the respondent's identity, which suspicion of the interviewer's motives may lead him to deny. Thus, as Goode and Hatt[1] recommend, the interviewer should

[1] Goode and Hatt, *Methods in Social Research*, chap. 13.

not explain when the door is opened 'I am looking for a Mr Smith'. If the person opening the door is an adult male, he should ask immediately, with a certain confidence, 'Mr Smith?' Identity is far less often denied, and Mr Smith is much more often at home, following the second approach. If, however, despite this precaution, the interviewer is asked 'Who wants him?', or it is claimed that 'He isn't here', especially if this statement is not amplified to suggest where Mr Smith might be, yet the interviewer strongly suspects that it indeed may be Mr Smith who is talking to him, he should immediately identify himself and explain his purpose. Often enough the respondent will then agree to the interview, perhaps hastily explaining that he thought the interviewer wished to make contact with 'the younger/older/other' Mr Smith.

Sometimes, before finally agreeing, the respondent may attempt to lay hands on the questionnaire, or try to read the questions, with such a remark as 'Well, let's see what you're asking – if it's up my street'. The interviewer should neither hand over the questionnaire nor attempt to hide it away, but can cap the respondent's remark with, for example: 'I haven't found anyone who found these questions much bother. You'll soon see. Let's go over a few. Actually, a lot of people soon find they're quite interesting.' Thus, the impression of secretiveness is avoided and the respondent's curiosity aroused.

CONDUCTING THE INTERVIEW

Once permission is granted, the nature of the technical problems facing the interviewer changes somewhat. It must be stated again that the interview is not a conversation. The interviewer and respondent should get on well together, but not *too* well. If some kind of chummy, chatty relationship springs up, the interviewer may become so engrossed in the respondent's replies that he neglects the task of completing the schedule. Much worse, he may be drawn into talking about himself and his own opinions and ideas. Yet if the interviewer thrusts relentlessly forward with the questions, the essentially asymmetrical form of the interviewer–respondent relationship becomes apparent, evoking associations with the relationships between a policeman and a suspect or a prosecuting counsel and the defendant.

48

Social and technical interviewing skill are required to steer between these two dangers. Let us consider firstly methods of avoiding excessive involvement with the respondent. The interviewer must be a good listener, but he must be a systematic and critical one. He establishes initially that he is a good listener by employing so-called 'non-directive' techniques. Two of these in particular are worth mentioning quickly. The first is simply for the interviewer to repeat without any particular emphasis the last words of a response. This is equivalent to saying 'I see' or 'Go on'. The second technique is simply to nod. Nodding is an extraordinarily important method of 'channel-control' between two speakers, conveying a message of the kind 'I have understood all you've been saying and it is really my turn to speak now and comment on it, but what you're saying is so interesting I'd prefer to miss my turn and hear more, so please go on'.

In the present writer's experience, interviewers soon learn how to get the respondent talking. They are often less successful at getting him to stop and to consider a fresh topic without destroying some rapport. They have equal trouble refusing to be drawn into giving their own opinions.

Controlling the voluble respondent is sometimes little more than a question of withdrawing signals such as nodding or verbal remarks conveying interest. Occasionally, however, the interviewer must direct the verbal traffic more decisively. One tactic is to await a brief pause in the respondent's outpouring and remark 'What a pity there isn't time for you to tell me more about that. Let's turn to something just as important . . .' and then ask the next question. If some rapport is lost, and hence (perhaps) some information, this loss may be more than offset by the gain in information from being able to complete the schedule at all. Moreover, the voluble respondent is often voluble with other people, and therefore quite accustomed to being cut off gently at times.

If the respondent requests the interviewer's own opinion about some issue, the interviewer has no alternative but to be evasive. He might have to say 'Do you know, I've never thought about that properly myself. Anyway, what matters at the moment is what *you* think', or 'Hmmm . . . I'd have to think about that. Maybe I can give you my ideas in a moment, when we've finished.'

49

Another danger to carefully built-up rapport between interviewer and respondent is the so-called 'embarrassing question'. One is not necessarily thinking here about inquiries on obviously explosive issues such as criminal behaviour or sexual deviation: inquiries in such areas are for the accomplished interviewing expert only, and, as the Kinsey team showed, to undertake them successfully may involve a virtual inversion of normal interviewing rules.[1] Whether other kinds of inquiry cause embarrassment depends a lot on their context, but two areas where trouble often arises in more routine surveys are inquiries bearing on the respondent's social status or on his income.

It will be a great help to the interviewer if the official wording of the questionnaire allows some such introduction as: 'Now we would just like one or two simple facts about your own income. . . .' It often helps to present the respondent with a card upon which a number of income categories are offered for choice. He can then simply say, e.g., 'It's D' or 'That'd be number five'. In fact, the writer has found respondents more forthcoming on this particular issue than is sometimes suggested. However, frequently enough such an inquiry might well meet with: 'My income? Oh, I don't know about that. What's that got to do with it?' To which the interviewer can usually reply with absolute forthrightness: 'We aren't interested in *your* income as such. But you sometimes find that people's income may be connected with other things. Other times you can show there's no such connection, though people say there is. We have to be able to say one way or the other. This is really just a statistical question. Actual individuals couldn't appear in the analysis.'

Three other kinds of 'embarrassing' situations must be mentioned – repetition, inconsistency, evasion. The first is relatively easy to handle. Here the interviewer arrives at a question which has apparently been answered by a previous reply to another. Should he bother the respondent with an apparent 'repetition'? The methodological rule here is a categorical 'yes'. However, a brief introduction may be in order: 'We may have covered this, before, but all the same I'd just like to ask. . . .' Surprisingly often an important qualification to the previous

[1] A. C. Kinsey *et al.*, *Sexual Behaviour in the Human Male* (Philadelphia, 1948).

'reply' appears at this stage. Indeed, the reply may appear to contradict the previous statement. How should the interviewer handle this problem? Since this situation is analogous to that of evasion, we may at this stage introduce the technique of *probing*, which can cope with both situations.

PROBING

As noted, the interviewer must remain a *critical* listener. It is therefore his general duty to note and respond to contradictions or evasion in responses. The extent to which he may do so will depend on his own skill – to point out evasion and contradiction tactlessly may destroy rapport or lead to abortion of the interview – and the policy of the survey director. Some survey specialists permit interviewers to probe for factual information only. There is general agreement that successful probing requires substantial interviewing experience.

Evasion, let it be said, is often more apparent than real, and a usable reply is gained merely from repeating the question. The response 'Don't know' can stem either from ambiguous or vague question wording *or* from genuine lack of information or opinion *or* from deliberate evasiveness. For this reason, whether to press a question by repetition or probing is always a difficult tactical decision. Often the interviewer must simply judge for himself the respondent's general frankness.

Other kinds of evasion are more apparent. For example:

Interviewer: How well would you say you get on with your foreman? Would you say: Very well; pretty well; not so well; or very badly indeed?

Respondent: Oh, I don't see very much of him. He's all right I suppose.

This reply is evasive and slightly ambiguous. The interviewer decides to repeat the question:

Interviewer: I see. But how well would you say you get on with him. Very well; pretty well; not so well; or very badly indeed?

The respondent still resists, but indicates a tack for the interviewer to follow, which he does:

Respondent: He doesn't come around our part that much . . . maybe it's just as well.

Interviewer: It's just as well he doesn't come around the part of the factory where you are?

Respondent: You've said it.

Interviewer: Why is that, would you say?

Respondent: Well, it's the boys, isn't it? And his attitude. . . .

Interviewer: The foreman's attitude? How do you mean?

Respondent: Well, like he's a bit big-headed since he got made up. The boys, they hate his guts.

Interviewer: So the other people working there don't get on too well with him. What about you? Would you say you yourself got on very well; pretty well; not so well; or very badly indeed with him?

Respondent: Very badly indeed.

The general rules of probing can be seen from this example: first, repeat the question; second, summarise and reiterate the respondent's replies; third, request amplification ('How do you mean?'); fourth, request explanations ('Why is that?'). The general form is non-directive. Occasionally, however, probing must be more direct, and point out inconsistency, e.g.:

Interviewer: How many hours a week overtime do you put in on average?

Respondent: Oh, lots, lots . . . let's see, it'd be at least twenty.

Interviewer: At least twenty?

Respondent: Easily that, more some weeks.

Interviewer: I see. Now let me see if I've got this right. Earlier on you said you went to union branch meetings nearly every week. Do you ever find this overtime stops you going to a branch meeting?

Respondent: Oh yeah, it's bound to, isn't it?

Interviewer: About how often does it stop you going to branch meetings?

Respondent: Oh, quite a lot.

Interviewer: Quite a lot?

Respondent: Oh yeah.

Interviewer: About how often would you say?

Respondent: Well, actually it's stopped me going down the branch at all lately.

Interviewer: Since about when is that?
Respondent: Oh, about the last six months, since this big order.

Another type of probing may occur when some form of 'don't know' or 'can't remember' type of response has been given, yet (i) it is vital to have a more precise answer, and (ii) the interviewer suspects such an answer may in fact be available but that it simply cannot be recalled by the respondent (not that he is concealing it). Here the interviewer might rephrase the question, give examples, or attempt to lead the respondent back to the 'forgotten' fact or feeling. Suppose, for example, the respondent has said he cannot remember how old he was when he opened a bank account, but that it is vital to obtain this information exactly. The sort of tactic possible is suggested below:

Interviewer: It *is* easy for things like that to slip the mind. You say your first job was in London. Was that your home at the time?
Respondent: Well no, not at first. I was in Bexley with my parents, but you know what it's like at that age, and the travelling got a bit of a bind. So when I was – oh, 23 – yes 23, that was when Hitler went into Czechoslovakia, if I'm right – well about then I got a place in Battersea. It was a bit rough, but I was independent. I joined the old Territorials about then, like everyone I knew was. Not long after – bang – it's the war.
Interviewer: And you were called up?
Respondent: A turning-point in my life. The R.A. Being a Territorial helped, I suppose, but it wasn't long before I was commissioned – yes, that's when it was – I had to have it for mess bills and all that. . . .
Interviewer: The bank account. . . .
Respondent: Yes, I must have been, let's see, 25. . . .

The interviewer has secured this information initially by taking the respondent back to a time (leaving home) when a bank account might have soon become a necessary aid to independent living. As luck has it, the recollection of a rather different event precipitates accurate recall, but this is irrelevant. The form of the probe is essentially that of getting the respondent to relive aspects of his life potentially relevant to the

C

issue. However, such tactics bring us to the fringe of the therapeutic interview, and are decidedly the province of the more expert.

RECORDING

It is possible for an interview to be thoroughly successful in the sense that full and honest replies are achieved from the respondent, yet disastrously inadequate from the point of view of analysis because the interviewer has taken no care with his recording. Even with schedules in which simple closed-choice questions predominate, the interviewer can carelessly circle or tick the wrong boxes, or forget to tick some at all. It is therefore often a wise policy quickly to check that all questions that should have been answered in fact have been before leaving the respondent. Occasionally the interviewer may be able to spot possible misrecordings as he is doing this and check with the respondent while he is still with him.

In any case, the schedule should be reviewed as soon as possible after leaving the respondent. Before outlining the reasons for this, it is necessary to say something about the recording of answers to open-ended questions while the interview is still in progress.

The rule for answers to such questions is unambiguous: they should be recorded as far as possible verbatim as the respondent talks. It is recognised, however, that it is usually impossible to follow this rule to the letter. Even if the interviewer possessed shorthand, which he very rarely does, his need to listen sympathetically yet critically to the respondent's reply might jeopardise his ability to obtain verbatim quotes. What, then, can be done?

Firstly, there is no need to wait for the end of a reply before beginning to record it. It is rare for the respondent not to pause between the component thoughts of a long utterance. Furthermore, like nearly all of us, he will tend to repeat himself somewhat and to pad out the substance of his reply with numerous redundant verbalisms ('sort of', 'you know', 'by and large', 'see what I mean?', etc.). Unless it is absolutely essential that the entire structural qualities of his speech should be obtained, which is not common in survey research, there is no obligation on the interviewer to capture all of these. True, they

54

may indicate an emotional state relevant to the nature of the reply – for example, tension, indifference or conviction. If so, and the interviewer simply cannot record all of them, the next-best step is for the interviewer to make a note of his judgement of the emotional tone.

Secondly, although he lacks shorthand, the interviewer can certainly learn to abbreviate. Connectives such as 'and' and 'therefore' (or its equivalents) have commonly used symbols, and the indefinite and definite articles can usually be omitted entirely. Abbreviations for terms which crop up repeatedly in the discussion of key topics can be worked out, and vowels can be omitted from most words. Once the interviewer forces himself to pursue full quotation, such short cuts soon occur to him. This often virtually closes the gap between the speeds of delivery and recording.

Thirdly, if he still falls badly behind the respondent's flow, a legitimate expedient is for the interviewer simply to announce the fact ('I'm sorry, I didn't quite get that down right and it sounded very interesting'). Respondents usually repeat what they have said, flattered that the interviewer should have considered it so important. Often, incidentally, respondents will indeed spontaneously tailor their own rate of delivery to the interviewer's manifest capacity to follow: this can usually be read as a sign of the existence of good rapport.

When probing is used to prompt fuller replies to open-ended or other questions, the interviewer should indicate prompting questions on the schedule. The usual practice is to preface the probe used with either of the symbols

→ or ⊗, e.g.
⊗ Repeated question.
→ 'Why did you leave that job?'

Despite all these steps, absolutely full recording will probably not have been achieved. Consequently as soon as possible after taking leave of the respondent the interviewer should review the schedule. Business and pleasure may often be conveniently mixed by doing so over a cup of coffee or glass of bitter in any suitable nearby establishment. He will find, as he re-reads the schedule, that many unrecorded responses or indicative items of the respondent's (or his own) behaviour return vividly to him. Some of these (suitably indicated as editorial additions) can be incorporated in the schedule. If answers to some questions are missing, the replies can still usually be recalled at this stage, or inferred from other responses.

It is also sound practice for space to be provided on the questionnaire for the interviewer to write a brief report on the interview as a whole. This might include any problems he experienced in gaining consent, his assessment of rapport, and an estimate of the respondent's truthfulness. It may have been that the interview was disturbed by the presence of other people, a family row in the next room, children playing, a phone constantly ringing or a secretary bringing letters to sign.

These facts have an important bearing on the reliability of the interview as a whole. It is especially vital to note any behavioural or situational features of the respondent which were inconsistent with his report of his views, or his values or his circumstances: avid readers may be found in houses conspicuously devoid of books; housewives who claim they can never buy any new clothes are often most attractively turned out, even when the interviewer arrives unannounced; people who 'smoke hardly anything' may be found surrounded by dirty ashtrays.

One final problem of the interview situation itself may occur when the time comes to leave. With brief street interviews, a smile and a 'thank you' is quite sufficient. But especially if it has occurred in a private house and has included the more penetrative kind of questions on opinion and attitude, the respondent may be reluctant to let the interviewer depart immediately. For his own part, the interviewer may feel that a sudden departure unpleasantly violates the emotionally-laden fiduciary atmosphere surrounding rapport. And if the respondent is left with a feeling of unease and dissatisfaction from an abrupt rupture of the relationship built up over perhaps the previous hour and a half, he may report his experience adversely to other people. This will damage the reputation of survey research as a whole. Furthermore, he may know other people who are to be interviewed at a later date and cause them to refuse when the time comes for them to be approached. (If it *is* likely that the respondent knows other potential respondents, the interviewer should request him not to discuss the questions he remembers with them, since this might cause them to prepare 'good' answers.)

Again, there is no easy solution to this problem. Perhaps the best tactic is to introduce cues which hint at the approaching termination as the interview draws into its final stages. The interviewer can glance at his watch and quickly remark 'Well I mustn't keep you very much longer now, so for the last minute or so could I just ask you. . . ?' He might even apologise, after the last question, for hurrying the respondent because he has an appointment at a fixed time with another respondent. (He should not, ideally, have hurried him at all of course.) If such remarks are accompanied by sorting of papers and pocketing of pens and pencils, the respondent will already be half-reconciled to the fact of termination before more decisive farewells must be said.

In saying goodbye, the interviewer should be generous in his thanks for the respondent's time and co-operation and may repeat his original assurances of the value of the information that has been provided and the confidential manner in which it will be treated.

There has been no space here to deal with the survey director's role in ensuring adequate interviewing. For these matters, reference must be made to the suggested literature below. Clearly, however, interviewers should never be sent into the field without some prior training (in mock interviews) and thorough briefing in the survey objectives. Once completed schedules begin to arrive, they should be studied by the director for their adequacy of coverage and recording, and comparisons should be made between the performance of different interviewers. This, it should be emphasised, is particularly important in the early stages of the programme.

FURTHER READING

R. L. Kahn and C. F. Cannell, *The Dynamics of Interviewing* (New York, 1957).
R. K. Merton *et al.*, *The Focussed Interview* (New York, 1956).
F J. Roethlisberger and W. J. Dickson, *Management and the Worker* (New York, 1964) esp. pt II.

CHAPTER FIVE

The Use of Visits and Field Studies in the Teaching of Economics[1]

N. Lee

The justification for any aid in economics teaching must eventually rest upon the theory accepted of the way in which children learn economics. Visits and field studies have probably been both underused and misused in the teaching of economics because of confusion over what constitutes 'economic understanding' and the way in which it is acquired. We start, therefore, by briefly considering the way in which economic understanding is acquired in order to identify the appropriate role of visits and field studies in the teaching programme. This is followed by a discussion of their content and organisation.

THE LEARNING PROCESS IN ECONOMICS

The traditional view of learning is based upon the assumption that children require a considerable degree of maturity and an ability to manipulate high-level abstraction terms *before* they are in a position to undertake a systematic study of economic analysis. This view is commonly held by those who oppose the teaching of economic analysis at school level. According to this view, learning economics involves gaining familiarity with the main concepts of the subject and acquiring an understanding of the logical relationship between them and the further implications which may be deduced from these relationships. In such a scheme of things, visits and field studies have no obvious central place: at most they are seen to have a peripheral role in the teaching of applied economics.

More recently an alternative view has been advanced, developed from certain ideas of Piaget and Bruner.[2] It ques-

[1] An extended and modified version of 'Visits and Field Studies', in N. Lee (ed.), *Teaching Economics* (Economics Association, 1967).

[2] N. Lee and H. Entwistle, 'Economics Education and Educational Theory', ibid.

tions whether 'maturity' and ability to manipulate high-level abstraction terms are mainly a function of age and ability. 'Maturity', it would argue, is dependent also on the degree of previous exposure of the pupil (in school and outside) to economic situations and experiences; 'ability to manipulate concepts' in economic analysis is mainly dependent upon an appreciation of the relationship between each concept and the multitude of concrete situations from which the concept (by process of abstraction) has been derived. The learning process is therefore seen in terms of the following sequence:

Experience of particular economic events → abstraction of the peculiar features of particular events → derivation of the concept which contains some or all of the common features of all the events observed → the incorporation of the concept (together with other concepts similarly derived) into an analytic system → derivation of implications of analytic system → application of analytic system (and its implications) in the interpretation of new economic situations.

The reader will notice that this sequence not only implies a different explanation of the learning process, it also implies a reduced emphasis on the *a priori* analytic method. In line with more recent thinking, greater emphasis is placed upon economics as an empirical science in which the analytic system is evaluated according to its ability to convey understanding of existing economic situations and accurately to predict the consequences of changes in elements within those situations.

If this alternative view of the learning process is accepted, then two points of importance for the content of this chapter emerge:

1. Economic education, especially at the introductory stages, must be more heavily involved than it has been in extending pupils' experience of concrete economic situations.

2. This extension of experience must be closely integrated into the process of understanding economic analysis and should not be treated as a separate, descriptive component of the economics course.

What follows is implicitly based upon an acceptance of these two points.

The Nature and Distinctive Contribution of Visits and Field Studies

A pupil's experience of concrete economics situations can be built up in a number of different ways: by drawing upon the teacher's own experience, by the regular reading of a 'quality' newspaper, by the use of case studies based upon actual situations, by exposure to visual material through films, film strips and television. In general these sources are under-utilised, though considerable discrimination is required in selection because of their uneven quality. The visit and field study do help to fill some of the gaps in the supply of suitable written and visual material. However, their *special* value is in giving pupils first-hand experience through direct observation of the economic institutions and situations they are studying. Apart from the benefits arising from the directness and the immediacy of the occasion, pupils are able to obtain far greater information on a particular situation than they could normally hope to acquire from secondary sources. This, however, in inexperienced hands can be a mixed blessing – the task of separating the wheat from the chaff is a matter to which we shall return shortly.

On close examination it is remarkable how extensive is the scope for using direct observation as a learning instrument in economics. In this respect economics is at an advantage over a number of the more traditional subjects in the curriculum – though this is not widely appreciated nor greatly exploited. Most frequently *visits* are arranged to factories belonging to an industry involved in the examination syllabus – for example, a motor-assembly plant, a coal-mine or a cotton-spinning mill. Less frequently, visits are arranged to distributive outlets or transport undertakings as part of a study of the retail trade or the transport industry. Yet such types of visit need not be linked to the descriptive study of a particular industry. Instead a visit could form an integral part of teaching the theory of the firm, in which case additional information would be sought on the decision-making process in the firm as it affected such matters as price, output, location, investment and advertising. In a similar way an industrial visit could be arranged to obtain additional information on labour relations and collective bargaining machinery in order to form an integral part of the teaching programme on wage determination.

Apart from industrial and commercial visits there are also visits to financial and political institutions to consider. The Stock Exchange visit is a popular example in the first category which, depending upon the teaching object in mind, could be used as part of a study of business finance or of price determination in a highly competitive market. Similarly a carefully chosen visit to Parliament or a local authority meeting might form part of a teaching programme dealing with some aspect of the role of government in economic affairs – for example, investment in the nationalised industries, financing the social services or financing local services.

The *field study* is a teaching technique borrowed from geography and is used to encourage pupils to observe and identify the operation of economic forces within a specified geographical area. It may involve visits to a number of separate economic units, but its essential characteristic is its examination of the relationship between units in their spatial setting.

There is a growing view that economic analysis has unduly neglected the spatial dimension of economic activity and that a number of major problem areas – regional imbalance, urban renewal, traffic congestion, pollution – have received insufficiently thorough attention by economists as a consequence. The field study, by making the spatial dimension explicit in the teaching programme at the 'grass-roots' level, would seem to offer pupils the opportunity to extend their concrete experiences in the spatial dimension upon which a better understanding of locational and regional analysis could be built.

A field study is normally more extensive than a single visit and a greater allocation of time is needed for it. In some schools a whole week is set aside for this purpose.[1] This type of field study and, to a lesser degree, the normal type of industrial visit can cause timetabling problems, though these are not insuperable. At the same time it is worth noting that certain types of field study can be carried out quite satisfactorily within the normal timetable if undertaken in the close vicinity of the school or college.[2] The most obvious opportunities for observing

[1] See Chapter 15 below; also B. R. G. Robinson and D. N. Eltringham, 'Economics Field Studies in Schools', in *Economics* (autumn 1966).

[2] P. G. Cox, 'Economics Field Studies in Schools', in *Economics* (spring 1967), and E. G. West, 'Economics Without Tears, I', in *Economics* (1957).

economic forces in action are often the most easily overlooked – the local market or auction, land use in the vicinity of the school, traffic congestion in the High Street.

The starting-point in an economics field study is defining a geographical area (urban, village or rural) and identifying its land-use pattern. From this point the study could develop in a variety of directions depending upon the type of pupil and the time available. Are there observable patterns in land use: for example, is land in different parts of the urban area devoted to different purposes – office, industrial, retailing, residential, etc.; how are these specialised land-use areas related to each other; are certain areas of land more intensively used than others (high-rise compared with low residential density areas) and where are these areas located? What are the main features of the transport system, the major traffic flows and their origins and destinations? After description, attention inevitably turns to analysis and explanation and this would involve elucidating the concept of a land market and the forces operating through that market in determining the structure of land prices. An alternative approach might be to pose the question: do the prices of land/houses/products vary from one part of the town to the other? Collection of data on spatial price differences would, at the analysis level, involve adapting the single market-price equilibrium concept to account for differences in market price in spatial equilibrium.

These illustrations are sufficient to indicate that far from being solely an 'easy introduction' to an elementary piece of analysis, both the field study and the industrial visit can form an integral part in the teaching of quite complex economic theory. The benefits, at different levels of teaching economic analysis, are potentially considerable: however, these benefits are not always realised in practice. Far from stimulating interest in study, a visit can easily be treated as a school trip of an extra-curricular nature. It may simply involve being 'shown round the works' in order to view the technical processes of production. The groups may be too large for all to hear the narrative of the guide who, in any case, may be unqualified to answer the types of questions economics students should be asking. Because the visit is short the understanding acquired may be very superficial and the features observed on the visit may be misleading if they are not typical.

62

More correctly, however, these shortcomings are features of the badly organised visit and for the most part could be avoided by adequate forward planning. The principal matters that require careful attention when planning a visit are listed below. No doubt a similar list could be prepared for a field study:

1. *The purpose of each visit*. The type of information and understanding it should elicit and the precise way in which it will fit into the teaching programme should be clear in the teacher's mind at an early stage in the planning process. This will be necessary before selecting the most suitable firms and institutions to visit.

2. *Restrictions imposed by the firm*. These should be ascertained at an early stage and will normally relate to such matters as the maximum size of the party, the minimum age of pupils, whether female pupils can be included and, possibly, instructions on suitable clothing and footwear.

3. *Arrangements with the firm*. Apart from such obvious arrangements as the timing and length of the visit, the co-operation of the firm should be sought in three principal matters:

(*a*) factory tours should be undertaken in sufficiently small groups (if necessary, offering to reduce the size of the party to make this possible);

(*b*) the visit should not be restricted to the production department but should include contact with personnel in those departments relevant to the purpose of the visit – labour relations, finance, costing, marketing, as the case might be;

(*c*) the provision of a reasonably quiet room in which questioning and discussion can take place without the competition of background machinery noise.

The initial arrangements can be undertaken by correspondence, but at some point personal contact either by telephone or, better still, a short preliminary visit by the organiser, is invaluable.

4. *Preliminary briefing of pupils*. Apart from communicating to the pupils the organisational details of the visit, this is the stage at which the purpose of the visit and its relation to the teaching

programme should be made clear and background information supplied which has not already been imparted as part of the normal teaching programme. It is an open question how far the teacher should detail the types of information the pupils should collect. Ideally, instructions should not be very detailed since this will cramp the initiative of the pupils. On the other hand, detailed guidance may be initially necessary for those with no experience of visits and possessing little background knowledge in economics. The gathering of information may be on an individual basis or in groups where particular tasks are assigned to individuals. In either event pupils should normally be equipped for taking notes during the visit.

5. *Reporting and recording the visit.* Once the visit has been completed, the lessons learned from it have to be made explicit and recorded in written form. Initially this may involve a reporting-back and discussion stage in which the main points of substance are identified and, under teacher guidance, their broad applicability and connections with the main teaching programme are identified. On this basis each pupil should then be in a position to prepare his own permanent record of the visit.

An Illustrative Outline for an Industrial Visit

Both when arranging a visit and when briefing the pupils the teacher must know the main types of information that are to be sought. As already indicated, this will vary according to the precise purpose of the visit and the educational background of the pupils on the visit. The outline below is included for illustrative purposes[1] to indicate the main topics upon which information might be sought by a group of intermediate-level students making a broad study of an industrial firm. Many studies will be more specialised and would deal with one or two topic areas which might be treated in correspondingly greater detail.

1. *Organisational structure and standard decision rules.* Legal status, number of establishments owned, major departments. How are the goals of the firm determined – are they always

[1] Alternative suggestions are contained in E. E. Lowe, 'The Organisation of Educational Visits in Factories', in *Economics* (1949), and N. Skene Smith, 'Questions for Business Visits' in *Economics* (1953).

consistent with profit maximisation? How are major decisions taken on such matters as pricing, product range, investment and advertising?

2. *Products and technical processes.* What is the range of products produced? What are the main materials used and how are they processed?

3. *Growth.* What has been the growth record of the firm? Has the growth rate been irregular – what have been the causes of this irregularity? What *forms* has growth taken – to what extent has diversification and/or vertical integration taken place? Why has the firm chosen to grow in this particular way?

4. *Location.* Where are the establishments of the firm located? What were the original reasons for these locations? Do these reasons still apply?

5. *Inputs and costs.* What is the present size and structure of the firm's labour force? What is its present capital structure? How does the level of total cost vary as output varies with existing plant? Is there any evidence of economies or diseconomies of large-scale production?

6. *Marketing.* What are the main cost elements involved in marketing? What information is there of the impact of different methods of marketing on sales? How are prices determined and in what circumstances would they be altered?

The emphasis in this outline is deliberately placed on economic rather than technical matters and on explanation to supplement simple description. A certain proportion of this type of information can only be supplied by fairly senior executives within firms and this raises difficulties of its own.

The time of senior executives is very valuable and is not always available at the time of a visit. One method of dealing with this aspect of the visit is to make separate arrangements to tape-record the replies of the senior executive to a detailed questionnaire at a time which is convenient to him.[1] The tape-recording could be played during the report and discussion stage in the classroom and its main points could be incorporated into the individual pupil reports. The tape could be accommodated in a tape-recording library for later use by other groups of students.

[1] A. H. Charnley, E. K. Grime and E. W. Lewis, 'A Library of Tape Recordings', in *Economics* (spring 1962), and E. G. West, 'Economics Without Tears', II, in *Economics* (1958).

There is also the problem of confidentiality of information. Certain of the types of information referred to above could prejudice the commercial interests of a firm if they became widely known, and some firms are understandably reluctant to divulge such information to pupils. Where this is so, senior executives should be encouraged to divulge the principles they employ (for example, in pricing or advertising), illustrating their points with hypothetical rather than actual data.

CONCLUSION

In discussing any teaching aid there is a temptation to make exaggerated claims on its behalf – a panacea for all teaching ills. The case which has been advanced in this chapter relates to a *particular* type of visit and field study which forms an integral part of a teaching programme in economic analysis and its applications. Other types of visit, which are frequently time-consuming irritants to all concerned, can be ignored without any great loss. Furthermore, the schools which can arrange their teaching programme on the assumption of weekly visits are in a small minority.[1] For the great majority of schools the extension of pupils' experience of concrete economic situations will have to be mainly achieved by the use of case-study material supplemented by visual aids. However, it would be a sad reflection on a teaching programme if it failed to provide pupils with *some* opportunity to gain first-hand experience of the operation of economic forces within their own environment, and then enlist this, in developing their understanding of the economic system, within the classroom.

[1] J. Harvey and L. Bather, 'Economics Subjects in the Sixth Form', in *The Times Educational Supplement*, 29 Apr 1960.

Part Two

Case Studies

CHAPTER SIX

Pricing in a Perfectly Competitive Market[1]

Myron L. Joseph

AIMS

Students often have difficulty in accepting the concept of a price fixed by market forces. The root of this problem is not usually the algebra or geometry used to develop the model of a perfectly competitive market, but the apparent unreality of some aspects of the model, which emerge when the student compares it with the 'real world'. In particular, it is part of most students' experience that the seller sets the price at which his product is sold. Given this, he is likely to argue that it is unrealistic to assume that the firm must accept the market price as given.

Consequently, even though it may be accepted that the market price equates supply and demand and clears the market, the conclusion is likely to be drawn that the model is an intellectual exercise with no application outside the classroom. Thus, a foundation has been laid for a misunderstanding of, and a resistance to, elementary micro-economics.

The case aims to avoid this barrier to understanding by giving students a chance to participate in the determination of market price in a highly simplified market. Subsequent comparisons of alternative market structures and analysis which assume price determination in competitive markets will then be based on a more solid foundation.

LEVEL AND REQUIREMENTS

'A' level, first-year degree, H.N.D. and H.N.C. in business studies and various professional courses.

About twenty-five to fifty students and at least two staff.

[1] This contribution is a rearrangement and slight modification of 'Role Playing in Teaching Economics', in *American Economic Review*, LV (1965), reproduced by kind permission of the author and the editors of the *Review*.

As the case can be noisy, an isolated classroom, or one which is available when other rooms are not in use, is ideal. To allow buyers and sellers to mix, furniture should be pushed back to the walls.

Materials needed are two packets of differently coloured 2 in. × 1 in. index cards, for the buying and selling instructions, a duplicated sheet of general instructions for each student (optional), and a blackboard, or, better still, overhead projector.

The case can be completed within a one-hour teaching period, but more time is required for variants and follow-up discussion.

NECESSARY PREPARATORY WORK

No particular preparatory work needs to be undertaken by the class; the case can precede or follow a conventional treatment of pricing in a perfectly competitive market.

The teacher will need to prepare in advance a set of buy and sell instructions. The instructions are based on demand and supply functions that intersect at a price of 180p per bushel. As can be deduced from Table 6.1, at the equilibrium price 24 transactions are possible and 8 buyers and 8 sellers are excluded from the market.

TABLE 6.1

Distribution of buy and sell instructions

Price (p)	Buyers (not more than the price)	Sellers (not less than the price)
280	4	–
260	4	2
240	4	2
220	4	2
200	4	2
180	4	4
160	2	4
140	2	6
120	2	6
100	2	4

The instruction cards will contain an order to buy 1000 bushels of wheat *at not more than* the specified price; or to sell

1000 bushels of wheat *at not less than* the specified price. To distinguish between buyers and sellers, the two packs of instruction cards should each be a different colour.

If required, copies of the following general instructions can be duplicated for distribution to participants.

You are about to participate in the operation of a commodity market. You will be given an order to buy or sell 1000 bushels of wheat under certain conditions. In general you should not reveal your instructions to any of the other dealers, unless you have a particular reason for doing so. You should consider yourself to be an agent, acting on behalf of a client who has given you specific instructions. You have an obligation to do as well as you can for your client, and you are not permitted to violate the instructions.

When the market opens, at the signal of the instructor, you may proceed to carry out your order. Buyers will be identified by a (red) and sellers by a (white) instruction card. A transaction is completed when a single buyer and a single seller agree on the terms of a sale. As soon as you complete a transaction, report to the instructor so that he may record and report your transaction. As soon as your transaction is reported, you should turn in your buy or sell order and receive a new one of the same kind. You may proceed immediately to complete a new transaction in accordance with your new order. If you are unable to complete a transaction within ten minutes, you may obtain a new order from your instructor.

When the market is closed, the instructor will determine and report whether the buyers or sellers have represented their clients more successfully.

THE CASE STUDY

Students are divided into buyers and sellers and given copies of the general instructions. One teacher, A, takes responsibility for distributing the buy and sell instructions and the other, B, records the prices at which transactions occur. Before starting the case, it is useful to run through the instructions verbally with students, stressing the importance of keeping to the rules and of acting in the best interest of their clients.

Once the case has started, students are free to circulate and make purchases and sales at any time, provided these are consistent with their client's instructions. On completion of a sale, it is reported to teacher B, who records it on the blackboard or the overhead projector, and announces the price. The two students concerned then give their old instructions to teacher A and receive replacements.

Some of the buy and sell orders should be retained initially and given out when instructions are returned. So that students will not know which transaction a particular order was used in, the instructions should be shuffled from time to time. This process minimises fluctuations in market conditions, although some shifts will inevitably be caused by the lag in reporting the sales and feeding orders back into the market.

After a short period of transactions at widely scattered prices, the market moves rapidly towards the equilibrium. In Table 6.2 a typical distribution of transactions over the range of possible prices is shown. It will be noticed that the prices which occur most often are clustered around the equilibrium price, which is what we would expect given our supply and demand functions.

TABLE 6.2

Distribution of transactions

Price (p)	Number of transactions
260	1
250	–
240	1
230	–
220	6
210	1
200	15
190	25
180	27
170	20
160	16
150	13
140	5
130	1
120	3
110	1
100	1

It will be found that students take their roles seriously, bargain vigorously and are keen to know whether buyers or sellers have best represented the interests of their clients.

One way of following up the case is to ask students to discuss the differences between their market and that specified in the perfect competition model. Given the background provided by the case, students are more able to evaluate the importance of such influences as information, factor mobility and product homogeneity in the market process. Additionally they appreciate why a firm in a perfectly competitive market will not deviate from the going price.

Problems of Application

If many students complete transactions at about the same time, teacher A may become surrounded by students all clamouring for new orders. This disorder can be minimised by arranging the furniture so as to separate buyers and sellers wanting new orders.

Some students will, of course, have received instructions which cannot be met at the market price. It is to prevent such students from cheating so as to remain in the market that it has been found useful to allow an order to be replaced if no transaction is possible within ten minutes. To improve motivation and reduce cheating, every opportunity, including the wording of the buy and sell instructions, should be taken to stress the importance and nature of the broker relationship.

Variants

All the transactions for a ten-minute period can be recorded on a separate section of the blackboard or the projector. This enables students to see the changing distribution of prices over time, and tends to speed the movement towards equilibrium price.

A change in the equilibrium price can be introduced by having a further set of buy and sell instructions based on a shift in the supply or demand function. These can be introduced into the case at an appropriate stage, one or both of the original sets of instructions being withdrawn. If this is done, the new instructions should be colour-coded so as to avoid accidentally reintroducing an instruction from the previous supply and demand functions.

73

CHAPTER SEVEN

Oligopoly Pricing[1]

Myron L. Joseph

AIMS

The pricing problems of large firms are remote from the experience of 'A'-level or undergraduate students. The aim of this role-playing exercise is to enable students to experience the instability of an oligopoly and the pricing problems faced by a firm with a small number of large competitors. Through participation, students learn of the strong temptation to cut price when fixed costs are high, and of the impact of price competition on oligopoly profits; they are also able to *feel* the pressure to collude.

LEVEL AND REQUIREMENTS

'A' level, first- or second-year degree, H.N.D. and H.N.C. in business studies and various professional courses.

A minimum of three participants, but preferably at least nine; the direct participants need to be a multiple of three, but the one or two students in excess of a multiple can assist the teacher in collecting data and recording results.

No special materials are required, only ordinary writing materials and blackboard.

The study can be completed within a normal teaching period, but more time is required for variants and follow-up discussion.

NECESSARY PREPARATORY WORK

No particular preparatory work needs to be undertaken by class or teacher; the exercise could precede or follow a conventional treatment of oligopoly pricing.

[1] This contribution is a rearrangement and slight modification of 'Role Playing in Teaching Economics', in *American Economic Review*, LV (1965), reproduced by kind permission of the author and the editors of the *Review*.

As background for the experiment, the teacher describes an industry with three identical firms competing for the market. The demand for the product is assumed to be relatively in-elastic, and marginal production cost is assumed to be low relative to the prevailing price, and constant. The teacher explains that firms can choose to sell at a high (H) price of £4, or at a low (L) price of £3. Under these assumptions the class estimate in a general way the likely distribution of sales among the firms for each combination of high and low prices. Then, using an explicit cost function (cost = £65 + sales × £1), they calculate the profit that would result from each price pattern. The sales and profits alternatives for all combinations of high and low prices are presented in Table 7.1.

TABLE 7.1

Sales and profits for combinations of high (£4) and low (£3) prices

Price combination	Price	Sales units	Profits £	Price	Sales units	Profits £	Price	Sales units	Profits £
HHH	H	30	25	H	30	25	H	30	25
HHL	H	10	−35	H	10	−35	L	80	95
HLL	H	5	−50	L	50	35	L	50	35
LLL	L	36	7	L	36	7	L	36	7

Costs = £65 + Sales × £1.

A simplified table showing only the profit alternatives for different price combinations is placed on the board. The class is arranged in groups of three, each student representing a single firm. Students are asked to study the profit possibilities and to try to make as much money as possible for their respective firms through a series of fifteen or twenty price-setting (high or low) decisions. The instructor promises to identify the most successful businessman in the class at the end of the experiment. The students within each group are instructed to make their price decisions independently and without any communica-tion. After each of the three has selected and noted a price, they are told to reveal the decisions to each other and to record the profits they have earned as indicated by the table on the board. This procedure is repeated until the experiment is concluded.

One-third of the groups are asked to set the initial price for all firms at the high level, one-third at the low level, and one-third are not given any binding initial conditions. The predominant result is that all three firms are forced into the low-profit alternative. Most of the groups that started selling at the high price fall off the plateau and are unable to return to it. The other groups are rarely able to attain the uniform high-price structure. The students are asked not to communicate. After the students have made about fifteen to twenty price decisions, the experiment is terminated and the frequency of different price patterns reported to the class. The experiment is then repeated with instructions permitting the students in each group to communicate freely before each price decision. Under these conditions a majority of the groups usually succeed in maintaining a uniform high-price level for the majority of the price decisions. But a substantial number are unable to collude or find that their agreements break down after a few decisions.

These are not controlled experiments, and the author makes no claim that they shed any light on the behaviour of oligopoly price-makers. But they do give the students an intense experience that makes the economic analysis of oligopoly behaviour more meaningful. The students can analyse the experimental conditions and assess the importance of demand elasticity, product substitution, communication, the cost function and their motivations in explaining their role behaviour. They see collusive agreements break down and feel the frustration of not being able to raise a price when it is clearly in the interest of all firms in the industry to do so. After their experience it is not difficult for them to understand the role of a price leader or the significance of tacit collusion. The experiment and the discussions that follow provide a dramatic background for the analysis of anti-trust policies in a learning context very different from the traditional authoritarian presentation of subject-matter. An experience of this kind helps to break down inhibitions and communication blocks in the classroom. The entire course gains through increased interest in the subject-matter and the student's involvement in the learning process.

VARIANTS

As an alternative or repeat role-playing exercise, or as a written exercise, the experimental conditions of demand elasticity or of cost function can be changed. Thus a cost function with lower overheads and higher unit costs, which, in the example below (Table 7.2), gives the same profits for the combination HHH, clearly reduces the extremes of profit and loss and thereby both reduces the pressures to collude but also the incentive to deceive by breaking a high-price agreement which the other two firms are keeping.

TABLE 7.2

Sales and profits for combinations of high (£4) and low (£3) prices

(Alternative formulation with lower overhead and higher marginal costs)

Price combination	Price	Sales units	Profits £	Price	Sales units	Profits £	Price	Sales units	Profits £
HHH	H	30	25	H	30	25	H	30	25
HHL	H	10	−5	H	10	−5	L	80	55
HLL	H	5	−15	L	50	25	L	50	25
LLL	L	36	11	L	36	11	L	36	11

Costs = £25 + Sales × £2.

CHAPTER EIGHT

A Survey of a Local Used Car Market

D. J. Hancock and D. P. Gabriel

AIMS

The project outlined in this chapter was undertaken by students at Madeley College of Education at the end of the first year as an integral part of a three-year course designed not only to acquaint them with economics, but also to train them to be teachers of the subject. Considerable emphasis was therefore placed upon methodology. Intentionally the students carried out the project with only limited guidance from the staff, so that they would experience at first hand some of the difficulties and problems associated with conducting surveys. A change of emphasis to give greater weight to other aims would make the project more useful for teachers whose primary wish is to increase their pupils' interest in, and understanding of, economics. The first of these other aims is to discover the major influences upon the price of used cars and to examine the relevance of the textbook models of perfect and imperfect competition to the real world. It is then appropriate to study the structure and organisation of the industry: to investigate, for example, whether it is mainly in the hands of small traders or in those of larger joint-stock firms; to note if economies of scale exist and make themselves evident in lower prices charged by the larger units. Finally, if resources permit, it is interesting to study dealers in different areas to assess whether or not location has any significant effect. This list of aims can easily be modified to suit individual requirements, but a word of warning is necessary. Surveys of this nature can easily become too ambitious and much time and energy wasted in gathering more facts than can usefully be analysed.

78

The method of conducting the project places one important restriction upon the age of the pupils who may take part. While one group of pupils is interviewing the used car dealers, a second group has the task of checking on the results of the interviews by bargaining for the 'sale' of a car, or cars, which they possess or can borrow, with the dealers who have been interviewed. They thus have to be able to drive. Apart from this, any group of pupils or students who are old enough to travel around in pairs with safety can carry out the project. The level of economics being studied will determine the degree of sophistication of the survey; at elementary levels the aims would appropriately be restricted to analysing the structure and organisation of the used car trade, while at more advanced levels examinations of concepts such as imperfect competition would be the core of the exercise.

With a group of twenty pupils and two members of staff, a week is required for the completion of the project. Half of that time is devoted to interviewing and bargaining, the remainder to analysing the results and presenting the report. Two members of staff could expect to spend about three days making preliminary arrangements, but this time would be spread at intervals over several weeks. Twenty participants covering about forty dealers in an area with an average radius of ten miles from the base of operations would require about £20. The major items of equipment are the used cars. Four or five are necessary for a group of this size. In addition, stationery, clipboards with waterproof covers, duplicating equipment, maps of the area, and lists of dealers obtainable from local newspapers or telephone directories, together with a room to serve as a base, are all that is needed.

NECESSARY PREPARATORY WORK

Having obtained approval from the appropriate authority to carry out the project and sufficient funds on which to draw, the next step in the preparation is to select four or five suitable cars. In the interests of standardisation, cars of identical make and age are desirable. This ideal may be impossible to achieve and one may have to be content with cars of popular make and comparatively recent manufacture. Vintage Bentleys or highly modified sports cars should be avoided, as only specialist dealers may be interested in them. It is essential to check that insurance cover is adequate. Many insurance companies consider that taking in a project of this nature is equivalent to using a car for business purposes and demand extra cover. Since few car owners know the exact nature of their insurance, it is desirable to obtain written approval from the insurers to use the cars.

A choice of suitable dealers has then to be made, the number being dependent upon the resources available. Each one has to be approached personally, his co-operation sought and a time for an interview arranged. Telephone calls or letters are inadequate substitutes for personal visits as they tend either to be forgotten or ignored. Verbal arrangements should, however, be confirmed in writing.

The next, and most difficult, item to be prepared is the questionnaire to be used in the interviews. The framing of suitable questions is a highly skilled matter and teachers without expert knowledge should at least consult a book on the subject.[1]

The remaining preparatory work consists of the detailed planning of teams, timetables and routes to be used in conducting the survey and the allotting of tasks for the analysis of the results and presentation of the final report. Each member of the project should be presented with a set of instructions telling him exactly what he is to do and at what times. Detailed forms must be prepared for the recording of the answers from the questionnaire sheets to facilitate easy interpretation, and everyone taking part should know which part of the analysis and report is his responsibility. In meetings held during the preparatory period the aims and methods of carrying out the project, and the ways in which the results will be analysed and presented, must be fully discussed by all those taking part. Lastly it is advisable to notify the police that the survey is to take place so that they may soothe the fears of suspicious members of the public, and all those participating in the project should carry a letter identifying the holder as a member of a

[1] See Chapters 2, 3 and 4 of this book and the recommended further reading at the ends of these chapters.

team carrying out a survey with the approval of the proper authorities.

THE CASE STUDY

The progress of the project will naturally vary from case to case; the description that follows, based upon the experience at Madeley College, can therefore be only an approximate guide to what may happen elsewhere.

The project began on a Monday morning when five cars set out from College. Each car contained a team of four, two to conduct the interviews and two to 'sell' the car. The first pair were armed with their timetables and routes, and copies of the questionnaire attached to a clipboard protected by a plastic cover in case of rain. The questionnaire was divided into two sections. The first contained questions designed to discover the facts about the structure of the trade. We wished to know if the dealer was self-employed, in partnership, or a limited company; was he a single unit or a member of a group or chain; the number of employees of different categories; the range of activities undertaken; and so on. The second section was concerned with the pricing of used cars. We wanted to know if all the dealers used *Glass's Guide* (a catalogue of used car prices) and what factors had the greatest influence upon price, for example the age and mileage of the car, the condition of the bodywork, and so on.

To prevent dealers from associating the questionnaire with the students who were 'selling' their cars, the latter attempted to disguise the fact that they were students and only approached dealers either some two hours before or after they had been interviewed. It was felt that if dealers suspected that their answers were being checked, they might become less co-operative. Each team was given eight dealers to cover in two days, the Wednesday morning being held in reserve. It might seem that interviewing only two dealers each morning and afternoon is a leisurely pace, but the inevitable hitches which arose would have thrown a fuller timetable out of gear; in particular, bargaining could be very protracted. As it turned out our timing was correct as the Wednesday morning was required by several teams.

When all the outside work had been completed, the teams

81

returned to analyse the results. The members had been arranged into groups, each charged with analysing a different part of the survey. Each group was further expected to draw up a report of its analysis and conclusions, and to present this report to a general meeting of all those involved in the project. At this meeting, held on Friday afternoon, the whole project, its results and its shortcomings, was fully discussed. Finally, a general report containing an outline of the project and its conclusions was drawn up and duplicated so that everyone who had taken part had a copy for future reference.

The results of the first part of the survey were quite straight-forward and only an elementary knowledge of statistics was required to present the facts about the structure and organisa-tion of the trade in a clear and simple way. On the question of pricing our results were more problematic. Generally the accuracy of the answers to questions about price was confirmed by the experience of those who had tried to 'sell' the cars. Every dealer referred to *Glass's Guide*, which appears to be the bible of the used car trade, and prices between dealers varied by no more than 5 per cent from the highest to the lowest. The problems of interpreting these results will be discussed in the next section.

PROBLEMS OF APPLICATION

In planning this project, four major problems are likely to emerge. The first is to decide on clear and simple aims. Even in such a small and relatively specialised field as the used car trade there are a great many things which could be investigated, and it is essential to be ruthless in limiting the scope of the sur-vey to what is practicable with the available resources. It has already been noted that drawing up a questionnaire is a skilled task, and the best way to assess the questions is to try them out in advance on a few dealers not concerned with the major project. In this way at least the worst questions can be removed and important omissions noted. The third area of difficulty is in selecting suitable dealers and arranging interviews. It is necessary to have a sample which is representative of large, medium and small traders, and this can best be done by visiting the premises. Arranging interviews calls for a measure of tact. Some businessmen are suspicious of the purpose of surveys, but when this has been carefully explained, and anonymity promised, most are willing to co-operate. Generally arrangements are more difficult with large concerns as the man in charge is often not available and his subordinates are reluctant to take decisions in his absence. Finally, it is impossible to achieve complete standardisation of a procedure for 'selling' the cars since some people are better salesmen than others; the one precaution to take is to insist that the cars are 'sold' in isolation and not in part-exchange for another vehicle. This will reduce the price-dispersion problem. An important variant of this project would be to use only one car for 'selling', permitting better standardisation and more valid conclusions. It would, however, take much longer to visit forty dealers and the project would have to be reorganised to make the interviews and 'selling' sections independent of one another.

It is perhaps inevitable that some dealers will not be available at the appointed time when once the project has got under way. This is why it is essential to have some time in reserve. At this stage too, the deficiencies of the questionnaire will become apparent unless the worst of them have been removed by means of a pilot study. Otherwise, provided the planning has been efficient, conducting the survey presents few problems.

It is in interpreting the information relating to price that the greatest difficulties arise. The two main facts to emerge were that prices differed by very little between dealers and that all dealers based their offers closely upon the recommended prices in *Glass's Guide*. It is interesting to compare our results with those from a similar survey carried out in Chicago and discussed in pp. 1–4 of *The Theory of Price*, 3rd ed. (Collier-Macmillan, London, 1966) by G. J. Stigler. Our results appear to confirm Stigler's point that since consumers will push their search for better prices to the point where the cost of seeking more information equals the expected gains from the information, price variations are likely to be proportionately less for expensive articles than for cheaper ones.

The small price variation coupled with the use of *Glass's Guide* suggested another interesting speculation. Were all the dealers 'price-takers' in the textbook sense, and hence had we found a perfectly competitive market? Alternatively, if *Glass's Guide* arrived at their recommendations by consulting a few of the larger dealers, this would indicate that the market contained price leaders and was therefore imperfectly competitive. We had not included a study of *Glass's Guide* in our project and we were, in fact, unable to obtain information about it, so that we could not come to any definite conclusions; but the discussions which centred round this and other problems of interpretation proved to be valuable exercises in clarifying the meaning of economic concepts and exposing the complexities of the real world of economics.

CHAPTER NINE

Marley Company Ltd Plans to Increase its Export Market: A Role-Playing Case Study in Drama Form

R. F. R. Phillips

AIMS

This role-playing case study was devised for a Schools Conference of the London Branch of the Economics Association. A full day was spent at the London School of Economics with separate programmes for senior and junior pupils; of the latter there were 400. Some had studied up to 'O' level but a large number were just beginning their first economics course. As they had spent the morning with a lecture, brains trust and a film, it was essential in the afternoon to ring a change and attempt to obtain some form of participation and activity within a crowded hall of 400 students. A presentation in dramatic form of the problems of an export manager, it was hoped, would help the students to identify themselves with the manager. The play was divided into five parts and the producer introduced each part by asking questions verbally on what the student would do in the manager's position. To induce the student even further to take a part, even though of necessity only mentally, a questionnaire was cyclostyled and issued to each student. The major aim was therefore to induce the student to place himself in the role of a manager and to tackle the economic decision-making in a natural businesslike way.

As the students were mostly beginners, a secondary aim was to attempt to portray how a firm organises its managerial operations and to get the feel of a manager's work. The choice of the export market was partly governed by the topicality of the subject in 1969 and partly to introduce simple monetary problems.

D

LEVEL AND REQUIREMENTS

First-year 'A' level and second-year 'O' level.
A small stage or platform.
Five desks with placards to indicate names and functions of participants.
Five telephones (borrowed free from the Post Office).
Duplicated sheets for issue to students.

NECESSARY PREPARATORY WORK

An export manager from a large local firm was asked to take part (in this case Mr A. W. Risso-Gill of Marley Company). An hour's consultation allowed a skeleton to be prepared of the procedures and the points to be covered. A written outline was then sent to the subsidiary actors. The Board of Trade, Export Branch, provided a senior officer; Lloyds Bank Ltd provided from its headquarters an officer of managerial rank (Mr P. D. Briggs), who had been responsible for advising customers on the finances of exporting; United City Merchants consented to the use of one of their officers with accountancy qualifications (Mr D. G. Clowes). To have a schoolmaster on the stage who could, within the play itself, guide the discussion to pedagogic ends, a member of the Economics Association took the part of the Managing Director of Marley Company (Mr B. Williams of Sunbury G.S.). An hour's consultation clarified the role each was expected to play, and finally a rather longer brief was prepared for each participant. For the students, a programme of two foolscap pages was cyclostyled. This gave the names and roles of the actors, a brief outline of the purpose of the five parts of the play, a few statistical tables which would be used by the actors and two or three questions relating to the purpose of each of the five stages of the play. The five participants kindly sacrificed an hour to meet together in the morning of the play, to run over each one's role and the procedure.

THE CASE STUDY

The play had, as indicated, five stages. First, the organiser as compère introduced the speakers and described the work and set-up of Marley Company (helped by advertisement leaflets distributed to the pupils). His purpose, other than establishing the identity of the actors, was:

(a) to indicate the differences in the problems of marketing immediate consumer goods with a continuous flow, durable consumer goods where there is a need to find new customers and extend credit, and producer goods dependent on investment policy;

(b) to establish that Marley Company was a vertically integrated firm, with a complex managerial set-up and difficult problems of co-ordination and devolution.

The second stage involved a conference between the 'Managing Director' and the Export Manager of Marley Company (remember the former was a schoolmaster, although the latter was the real person). This aimed to establish why Marley Company was launching an export drive, and at the end of this stage – the conference on which they had been eavesdropping – the students had to abstract four main reasons and write them down. They knew before it started that this was the purpose of the conference. The two Marley Company officers also studied figures of past performances (which were also before the students) and a further set of questions drew the students' attention to the significance of statistics in guiding decision-making and gave them practice in reading statistics.

In the third stage the Export Manager explored potential markets and had conferences with Lloyds Bank, the Board of Trade and the United Merchants, to establish current price levels and whether the market had potentialities for expansion. Questions on the programme directed students to watch for price-elasticity and income-elasticity concepts at work. Again, use was made of statistical tables.

In the fourth stage, Marley Company, having selected two markets (Libya and Kuwait), explored the problem of market promotion. A conference with the Board of Trade officials and a conference with the United Merchants' representative highlighted the functions of the middleman. Questions directed the students to these problems.

In the fifth stage, the Export Manager faced the problems of financing the exports. The importance of credit and of interest rates as illustrated by the Bank Manager and Government assistance by the Board of Trade. The cost of the export drive to Marley Company and the need for liquid resources was the crux of the final conference between the Export Manager and his Managing Director.

PROBLEMS OF APPLICATION

The organiser is very much at the mercy of his actors. It is essential that the Export Manager should have a masterful personality and be thoroughly conversant with the teaching aims of the play. The other actors must be audible and must play to the Export Manager. It is important to ensure that actors are not long-winded, as this could easily divert attention to the work of their departments and away from the aim of the play. Both the Export Manager and the Managing Director saved the situation by firm interruption – the latter by use of his 'telephone' to the Export Manager. The play was over-ambitious. It worked the students at high pressure for an uninterrupted period of one and a half hours. At no time, however, was their attention lost and their teachers reported well on most of their written answers. The use of statistics in a realistic setting was particularly appreciated.

APPENDIX

Marley Company Ltd Plans an Export Drive: A Case Study in Drama Form[1]

Dramatis Personæ

		Phone	
Compère	R. F. R. Phillips		Economics Association
Marley Co. Managing Director	B. Williams	4	Economics Association
Marley Co. Export Manager	A. W. Risso-Gill	17	Marley Co.
Bank Manager	P. D. Briggs	55	Lloyds Bank Ltd
Board of Trade Official	R. E. Doubleday	600	Board of Trade
Export Merchant	D. G. Clowes	32	United City Merchants

[1] Apart from some minor amendments, this is the programme used at the Economics Association Schools Junior Conference, 25 September 1969.

Stage 1. The compère will introduce the speakers and give the setting

Question 1   On the Marley Co. brochures provided, mark with a tick those end-products which are producers' goods; with an X those which are durable consumer goods; with an O those which are immediate consumer goods.

Question 2   Marley Co. is an example of vertical integration because:

(*a*) its export department is independent of its production plants;

(*b*) its Export Manager is subordinate to the Managing Director;

(*c*) it has subsidiary companies overseas which are subordinate to the United Kingdom-based parent company;

(*d*) it has subsidiaries making the plastics, concrete, etc., which are its raw materials; plants which manufacture end-products; its own retail shops;

(*e*) it has a hierarchy of employees from labourers, skilled craftsmen, foremen, administrative officers to the top executives.

Tick the correct reason.

Stage 2. The Managing Director initiates a drive for more exports

Question 3   For what four main reasons is the managing director anxious to increase exports?

1.

2.

3.

4.

Question 4   Below is an abstract of statistics of a company's exports in £m., 1961–8. Why are the figures in the second line less than those in the first line after 1962?

	1961	1962	1963	1964	1965	1966	1967	1968
Sterling value	0·7	0·9	1·4	1·7	2·1	2·8	2·8	3·0
Adjusted to 1961 prices	0·7	0·9	1·2	1·4	1·6	1·8	1·9	2·1
Expressed as an index with 1961 as the base	100			200				300

Question 5   Fill in the missing figures on the third line for 1962 and 1966.

Question 6   In November 1967 the £ sterling was devalued by 14·3 per cent. This means that in 1966 to obtain £2·8m. sterling it would have to have earned, say, 2·8 m. units of foreign currency; after devaluation, however, it will need only 86 units of foreign currency to obtain £100 sterling.

(a) By how much has this company increased its receipts of sterling from export in 1968 as compared with 1966?

(b) By how much has this company increased or decreased its receipts of foreign currency from exports in 1968 as compared with 1966? (Assume that no countries except Britain have altered their exchange rates.)

Stage 3. Marley explores the problem of prices

Question 7   If North Africa is a more competitive market than Europe and if its people being poorer are more price-conscious, will demand in that market be more or less elastic than the European?

Question 8   The following figures are for carpet sales in 1000 sq. yds:

Price per sq. yd.	Sales
£2	6
£3	3
£4	1

If a company anticipates that its sales will vary with price as above and the cost at delivery remains constant at £2 per sq. yd., at which price will it prefer to sell: (a) at £4; (b) at £3; or (c) at £2?

Question 9   If the income elasticity of demand for carpets is 2 and the average income per head in North Africa is rising by 10 per cent per annum as a result of oil royalties, what sales may be anticipated next year if Marley price their carpets at £3?

Stage 4. Marley Co. examines the problem of market promotion

Question 10 State three main functions of the middleman
(United City Merchants).
1.
2.
3.

Stage 5. Marley Co. examines the problem of financing its exports

Question 11 (*a*) What is the current Bank Rate?
(*b*) Why does a rise in the Bank Rate deter Marley
Co.?
(*c*) On what security is Lloyds Bank ready to
lend?

Stage 6. Marley makes its decision

Question 12 (Your Homework)
What decision would you make?

CHAPTER TEN

A Case Before the Restrictive Practices Court: The Cement Makers' Agreement

M. S. Bradbury

AIMS

Under the Restrictive Trade Practices Acts of 1956 and 1968, most agreements between firms on such matters as prices, output and terms of trading must be registered with the Registrar of Restrictive Trading Agreements, who brings them before the Restrictive Practices Court. Such agreements are considered to be against the public interest and will be declared void, unless the parties to an agreement can prove to the Court that *both* of the following conditions are met:

(a) The agreement satisfies one or more of eight conditions specified in the Acts of 1956 and 1968 (often called 'gateways to the public interest').

(b) On balance, the benefits to the public resulting from the agreement outweigh any detriments (often called the 'balancing act').[1]

The case aims to inject realism into the teaching of the economics of imperfect competition, by encouraging students to apply the principles of economics to the analysis of a restrictive trading agreement. At the same time the need to decide whether 'gateways' have been established and whether the benefits of an agreement outweigh any resulting detriments, *before being told of the Court's decision*, encourages independent thought and provides a starting-point for an analysis of the Court's decision and an exploration of the extent to which legal institutions are an appropriate instrument for the control of

---

[1] See C. T. Sandford and M. S. Bradbury, *Case Studies in Economics: Economic Policy*, chaps 4 and 5, for a description of legislation in the United Kingdom on the control of monopolies, mergers and restrictive trade practices, and accompanying case studies.

restrictive practices. A subsidiary aim is to familiarise students
with economic source material.

LEVEL AND REQUIREMENTS

First- and second-year degree and H.N.D./H.N.C. in business
studies.

At least five students; as two students do not take a *direct*
part in stage 3, groups of less than five students may be too
small for spontaneous and sustained discussion. Conversely, too
large a group inhibits full participation in discussion.

The relevant law reports, e.g. one or more of the *All England
Law Reports*, the *Weekly Law Reports* or the *Restrictive Practices
Law Reports*, must be accessible. The basic source for this study
has been the *Weekly Law Reports*, vol. 1 (London, 1961) pp. 581–
608.

NECESSARY PREPARATORY WORK

Students should have completed an introductory course in
micro-economics and be aware of the main features of the legis-
lative and institutional framework within which the control of
restrictive trade practices is exercised in the United Kingdom.

The teacher should have studied the case selected in detail,
including comments on the Court's decision by economists.

THE CASE

Stage 1. About a week before the presentation of the case, one
student is asked to prepare a summary of the arguments presented by the Cement Makers' Federation in favour of the
major feature of their agreement; another student is asked to
summarise the detriments alleged therefrom by the Registrar of
Restrictive Trading Agreements.

The remaining students are each given a summary of background information and asked to write a short note on which
'gateways' and detriments they would expect to feature in the
case. The purpose of this exercise is, first, to ensure that all participants study the summary of background information before
the presentation; and second, to force students to look at an
agreement from the viewpoint of both the parties to it and the

93

Registrar. To help achieve this purpose, students may also be required to answer briefly, in writing, some questions on the background information. The notes and answers will help the teacher to predict difficulties or misconceptions which may arise in subsequent discussion.

A typical summary of background information might be as follows:

Summary of Background Information:
The Cement Makers' Agreement

The Demand for Cement

Cement is used to make concrete, mortar and cement products, which in turn are used in building and construction work. Consequently, the demand for cement is derived from the demand for constructional activities.

In 1961, in most markets there was no close substitute for cement and its cost was only a small proportion of the total cost of the constructional works for which it was demanded (slightly under 3 per cent on average). Indeed, it was claimed that punctuality and regularity of delivery might have a greater impact on total construction costs than small changes in the price of cement. The Restrictive Practices Court accepted that demand for cement was highly inelastic in response to changes of 5 to 10 per cent in the current (1961) price.

The growth of United Kingdom demand for cement (averaging about 4 per cent per annum between 1945 and 1961) was expected to continue. Fluctuations in aggregate demand in the economy were reflected in the demand for constructional activities and hence in the demand for cement. Export demand had fallen as local production displaced imported cement in the traditional Commonwealth markets.

The Supply of Cement in 1961

Portland Cement is made from calcium carbonate (which occurs naturally as chalk or limestone) and clay or shale. A mixture of these materials is fired in a kiln by pulverised coal or atomised oil to create a fused product called cement clinker. Cement clinker and gypsum are then mixed and ground to produce Portland cement. Whilst cement clinker can be stored, cement must be used soon after being made.

There are relatively few places in the United Kingdom where the retrieval of the raw materials needed to make Portland cement is economic. In 1900, 80 per cent of the cement used in the United Kingdom was made in the Thames and Medway areas. Three factors accounted for the dominance of these areas:

(a) Suitable chalk and clay deposits.
(b) Closeness to the markets of London and the Home Counties.
(c) Cheap sea transport for coal from Durham and to deliver the cement to other United Kingdom ports.

Since 1900, the emergence of road transport has eroded the cheap sea freights advantage enjoyed by the Thames and Medway areas, leading to increased production at 'inland' works, so that by 1961 only 32 per cent of United Kingdom production came from the Thames and Medway areas.

To benefit from economies of scale, new plants required an output of at least 200,000 tons per annum (compared with total United Kingdom sales of about 12 million tons per annum at the time of the case). Such plants had a capital cost per ton capacity of about £15 to £20 compared with about £12 to £15 for extending an existing factory.

As cement-making is a continuous process and fixed costs form a high proportion of short-run total costs, costs and profits are highly sensitive to small changes in output. It has been estimated that to operate a plant at 10 per cent below normal capacity would increase costs per ton by about 3 to $3\frac{1}{2}$ per cent and reduce profits by 20 to 25 per cent (at 1959 costs and prices).

The Cement Makers' Federation
In 1934, after a period of intense price competition in the cement industry, the Associated Portland Cement Manufacturers Ltd (A.P.C.M.) acquired the assets of a rival group which had become insolvent. At the same time, the Cement Makers' Federation established common pricing and marketing arrangements which ended price competition between members.

In 1961 the four groups and five companies which made up the membership of the Cement Makers' Federation accounted for almost all of the United Kingdom's output of Portland cement (imports were negligible except when temporary shortages occurred). The structure of the industry was as follows:

TABLE 10.1

Structure of the United Kingdom Portland cement industry in 1961

Producer	Market share* %	Number of separate works (total)	Number of works in Thames and Medway areas
A.P.C.M.†	62·0	29	12
Tunnel	12·0	3	1
Rugby	6·5	2 ⎫	1
Eastwoods	4·5	3 ⎭	
Remaining five companies‡	15·0	5	0

* Percentages of the total quantity of cement delivered in the United Kingdom.

† A.P.C.M. was the largest exporter. Two chemical companies which make cement as a by-product sell their output to A.P.C.M.

‡ One of the five companies is I.C.I., which produces cement as a by-product. Its output has been excluded throughout the case as its cost structure differs from the rest of the industry. One plant is owned jointly by Tunnel and one of the five companies. Data relating to two small Scottish producers of blast-furnace cement have also been excluded.

Source: Based on data in the *All England Law Reports*, vol. II (London, 1961) p. 82.

The major feature of the Cement Makers' Federation Agreement was the operation of a 'basing point' pricing system. Each works was treated as a 'basing point' for which a 'base price' was established, i.e. a price for cement delivered within a five-mile radius of the works. Concentric circles with radii in multiples of five miles were then drawn, each delimiting zones within which the delivered price increased the greater the distance of the zone from the works, until a price zone belonging to another works was intersected. In this way the whole country was divided into price zones.

On average transport costs accounted for about 18 per cent of the delivered cost of cement. However, these costs were not divided evenly between customers, or in proportion to the distance of the customer from the works. Instead, delivered prices increased less than proportionately with distance from the works, i.e. net of transport costs the producer received a lower price for his cement, the further the customer was from the works. Consequently, producers were encouraged to maximise local and minimise distant sales.

To help operate the agreement, the Federation established an independent costs committee, consisting of the Chairman of the Federation and an accountant, neither of whom had a financial interest in the industry. Each quarter, members of the Federation submitted details of their output, revenue and costs (not usually for individual works but for groups as a whole) to the costs committee. The weighted average costs and results for the whole industry (but not individual members) were then circulated to all members. If the costs committee or a member of the Federation considered that to maintain reasonable profits for the industry as a whole a change of price was needed, a meeting of the Council of the Federation, chaired by the independent chairman and attended by the independent accountant, was called to decide the matter. When fixing prices the general premise accepted by the Federation was that 'It is the function of the industry to provide the whole country with cement, whenever it is required, at prices and at places of delivery which bear a reasonable relationship one to another, and which provide a reasonable profit to members of the Federation not as owners of individual works or groups of works but taken as a whole.'

Stage 2. At the start of the presentation the teacher tells the remainder of the group that they are about to hear a summary of the case for and against the major features of the agreement, on the basis of which they will be asked to decide:

(a) Whether *in their view as economists* the Association has established that the agreement satisfies one of the 'gateways' specified in the Restrictive Trade Practices Acts of 1956 and 1968.
(b) Whether *in their view as economists* the Association has established that on balance the benefits to the public resulting from the agreement outweigh any detriments.

A typical summary of the case for the major feature of the agreement might be as follows:

The Federation contends that its agreement meets the requirements of 'gateway' (b) of the Restrictive Trade Practices Act, 1956 (section 21(1)(b)), i.e. confers specific and substantial benefits on the public as users of cement, which would not otherwise exist.

In an expanding industry under free competition (i.e. without the agreement) the long-run price level must be such that producers can attract the capital needed to build new plants. Given that the demand for cement is inelastic relative to the likely range of price changes, a price level sufficient to attract the capital needed to increase supply in step with demand is likely to exist.

As the risks associated with building a new cement works are reduced by the agreement, it follows that in its absence entrepreneurs would expect a higher return on capital, i.e. about 15 to 20 per cent. On the basis of the manufacturing costs at the lowest cost existing and at the newest works in the industry and using likely capital costs, the minimum prices per ton under free competition and the existing price are as follows:

TABLE 10.2

Estimated price per ton under competition and existing price (1959)*

	Lowest cost basis	Newest works basis
For 15 per cent return	133s. 1d.	137s. 0d.
For 20 per cent return	149s. 7d.	153s. 6d.
Existing industry	107s. 1d.	112s. 8d.

* These money values are expressed in old currency units as the data relate to a period before decimalisation.

Source: J. Tofts, in *Case Studies in Economics: Principles of Economics*, chap. 5.

Assuming that prices could not be reduced as a result of greater efficiency, the present prices are substantially lower than under free competition. This is because, in spite of the Federation's monopoly power, prices have been fixed which yield a return of slightly less than 10 per cent on a new works. Furthermore, the industries' investment plans suggest that members are willing and able to continue investing in new capacity as and when needed, at the present levels of prices and profits.

It is contended that the lower prices resulting from the agreement are a specific and substantial benefit to the public as users of cement.

A typical summary of the main detriments claimed to result from the agreement by the Registrar of Restrictive Trading Agreements might be as follows:

The agreement results in the following detriments:

(a) The adequate expansion of the industry has been prevented by discouraging the erection of new works in the most suitable geographical areas.[1]

(b) The price structure under the agreement is detrimental to buyers of cement for delivery close to the cement works, as the price includes a subsidy (estimated to be at most 7s. 8d. per ton) towards the transport costs of more distant customers, i.e. under free competition customers close to cement works would pay lower prices.

(c) Any such scheme of transport subsidy is detrimental to consumers, as it distorts the location of economic activity.

Stage 3. The group discusses the arguments and gives a decision. The two speakers should not take part in making the decision, apart from answering questions on specific points of detail.

Stage 4. The teacher discloses the actual judgement of the Court and explains how it was reached.

Stage 5. As a follow-up, the teacher can discuss comments made on the decision or on the operation of the Court by economists, e.g. R. Stevens and B. S. Yamey, *The Restrictive Practices Court: A Study of the Judicial Process and Economic Policy* (London, 1965).

PROBLEMS OF APPLICATION

To maintain interest and to keep within the time allocated for the case, the two student advocates must be able to speak in a

---

[1] The Court in fact rejected this detriment. Independent evidence suggested that at current prices, works at two locations considered most promising by the Registrar offered an inadequate return on capital.

clear, interesting and concise manner; a time limit may be useful.

The case must be kept within the limits imposed by its teaching purpose. In the case presented above, a considerable amount of detail has deliberately been omitted (e.g. no mention has been made of the aggregate rebate scheme operated by the Federation) so as to focus attention on the basing-point pricing system of the agreement. In practical terms this means that the teacher will have to give some guidance to the students presenting the case, on exactly what is wanted and on how to read the law report.

The remaining members of the group may ask for additional information to help them reach their decision. If the information requested was available to the Court, then it should be made available to the group (preferably by the two student advocates). But if the information requested was not available to the Court, the students should be told, and asked to reach their decision on what they will regard as inadequate data. In this way students are brought face to face with the realities of having to reach economic decisions with incomplete information. It may be useful to have the source material to hand during the presentation.

In August 1967 and November 1969 the National Board for Prices and Incomes reported on proposed increases in the price of Portland cement.[1] These reports not only update and amplify the economic data on the cement industry given in stage 1 of this case study, but also discuss the relevance of target rates of return on capital to price fixing. This information has been excluded from the 'Summary of Background Information', as it was not available to the Court. However, a discussion of the reports could usefully form part of stage 5 of the case study.

VARIANTS

In principle the method can be used to examine any case before the Restrictive Trade Practices Court – including those

[1] National Board for Prices and Incomes, Report No. 38, *Portland Cement Prices*, Cmnd 3381 (H.M.S.O., Aug 1967); National Board for Prices and Incomes, Report No. 133, *Portland Cement Prices*, Cmnd 4215 (H.M.S.O., Nov 1969). Students whose courses include Accountancy may be interested in the criticisms of the judgement in this case in A. Sutherland 'Economics in the Restrictive Practices Courts' *Oxford Economic Papers* (Nov 1965) pp. 386-98.

concerned with resale price maintenance, e.g. the Chocolate and Sugar Confectionery Case.[1] In practice it should be remembered that a case study is a means to an end and not the end itself. Hence only cases should be selected which illustrate points of economic significance. In particular, care should be taken to avoid cases which, though of legal interest, are of more limited economic interest.

An interesting variant of the case takes the form of a project. Students are asked to write short reports on particular features of a range of cases before the Restrictive Practices Court, or Monopoly Commission references, each of which is linked by a common theme. For example, a study of barriers to new competition could include student reports on cases involving aggregate rebate schemes, high marketing expenditure and brand proliferation, forward and backward vertical integration and economies of scale. A list of references and cases from which a suitable selection can be made will be found in any standard economic commentary on the Monopolies Commission and the Restrictive Practices Court.

[1] See *Case Studies in Economics: Economic Policy*, chap. 5, case 12.

CHAPTER ELEVEN

Industrial Location Decisions: Office Dispersal from Central London

M. S. Bradbury

Aims

In elementary economics, consideration of the spatial aspects of micro-economics is usually confined to examining the location decisions of firms in manufacturing industry. The rising importance of office relative to manufacturing employment and the interaction between office location decisions and the increasingly significant problems of urban and regional economics suggest that greater weight might usefully be given to office location. Furthermore, office location decisions are often less complex and closer to the students' experience than the standard examples drawn from manufacturing industry.

This case examines office location within the context of a firm with office accommodation in Central London which is considering moving to a suburban, regional or provincial site; the case has three main aims:

1. To give students an appreciation of the motives which lead firms to reconsider their office location decisions. When asked why firms might reconsider their location decision, many students suggest that in a market economy firms will be continuously driven to do this by the pursuit of profit and the forces of competition. The empirical data reproduced in Table 11.1 suggest that this view is a serious oversimplification.

    On the basis of similar data,[1] the Location of Offices Bureau has argued that 'A major distinction . . . is between firms which decide to move out as a planned method of achieving their objectives (expansion or economy) and those forced to make a decision by changes in external

[1] Location of Offices Bureau, *Annual Report 1965–6*, p. 29.

Table 11.1

Reasons for considering decentralisation 1963–70

Reasons for decentralisation	Number
Expansion	555
Economy	364
Expiry of lease and/or demolition	324
Integration with other parts of organisation	111
Staff recruitment	75
Traffic congestion	62
Staff welfare	32
Total	1523*

* Between the foundation of the Location of Offices Bureau in 1963 and the end of March 1970, the Bureau was consulted by 2220 firms, some of which gave no reasons for considering decentralisation and some of which gave more than one reason.

Source: Location of Offices Bureau, *Annual Report 1969–70*, p. 35.

circumstances (expiry of lease, demolition of offices). At the same time, a change in external circumstances frequently triggers off thinking about methods of cost saving, which leads on to a study of decentralisation possibilities.'

A useful by-product of following this aim is that several fundamental issues in the theory of the firm – e.g. the conflict between static and dynamic analysis – are brought to the students' attention, thus providing a gateway for future learning.

2. To point out the many forms which relocation can take. Students often assume that only one choice is available – i.e. between remaining in one office in Central London and moving to a new site in a development area. The case brings to the students' attention the choice between:

(*a*) central urban, suburban, regional and provincial locations;

(*b*) partial and complete moves;

(*c*) the dispersal of office activities between geographically separate offices and integration within one office (independently of location).

3. To develop an appreciation of the economic forces which

influence the choice between these various alternatives. A particular feature of the case is that it creates a foundation of 'experience' for subsequent teaching on external economies and diseconomies.

LEVEL AND REQUIREMENTS

'A' level, first-year degree, H.N.D./H.N.C. and various professional courses.

A convenient number of students is about twelve.

One copy per student of *Moving Your Office*, obtainable from the Location of Offices Bureau (L.O.B.). Students should be able to consult, as required, a recent L.O.B. annual report, the current edition of *A Wise Move* (L.O.B.), and a street plan of the City of London.

The case can be completed within two or three one-hour teaching periods, but more time is needed for variants and follow-up discussion.

NECESSARY PREPARATORY WORK

No particular preparatory work needs to be undertaken by the class; the case can follow, or preferably precede, a conventional treatment of the theory of location.

The teacher will need to prepare in advance duplicated copies of the memoranda described in the case.

THE CASE STUDY

Stage 1. About a week before the first classroom session, each student is sent a copy of the following memorandum:

Memorandum from Teacher to Students

Nonsuch Assurance Ltd
To all Planning Officers (Names of students):   From:

Office Accommodation

1. You will no doubt remember that six months ago the Board of Directors decided that a Corporate Plan should be prepared which would:

(*a*) set out the objectives to be pursued by the company for the next five years;

(*b*) propose how each part of the business could best assist the achievement of the company's objectives;

(*c*) outline the impact of (*a*) and (*b*) on the company's profits, annual investment, manpower, etc.

2. Following the preparation of the Provisional Manpower Plan, Mr Fox, the Manager of the Office Services Department, prepared a memorandum pointing out that we need to obtain extra accommodation if the manpower employed in our London headquarters offices is to expand as envisaged (copy attached).

3. At yesterday's Board meeting, I was asked to examine the office accommodation problem in the light of Mr Fox's comments and to suggest two alternative solutions, between which the Board will choose.

4. I should like you to join a working party to consider the matter. The first meeting will be on . . . at . . . in room . . . (date, time and place of next lesson).

5. Before then, you might like to consider the matter in the light of the enclosed booklet *Moving Your Office*.

(Teacher's name)

Director of Corporate Planning

(Date)

The following memorandum should accompany that of the Director of Corporate Planning:

Memorandum from B. Fox to Managing Director

Nonsuch Assurance Ltd

To the Managing Director:

(c.c. Director of Corporate Planning)

The Provisional Manpower Plan and Office Accommodation

1. I notice that the 'Provisional Manpower Plan' is to be considered by the Board at its next meeting. I have now read the plan and feel that I should point out some of its implications for our existing headquarters office accommodation in the City of London.

2. Originally all headquarters departments were housed in the same premises. However, the growth of the firm and our inability to expand on one site have led to our headquarters staff being accommodated in four separate offices as follows:

Location	Activity	Present staff	Five years' time
Threadneedle Street	Life and Fire Insurance, Pensions	200	270
Old Broad Street	Industrial and Motor Insurance	120	150
Throgmorton Avenue	Portfolio Management	20	25
Leadenhall Street	Marine Insurance	60	75
	Total staff	400	520

3. Except for our Theadneedle Street office, where ten more staff could be accommodated, all offices are fully utilised.

4. The lease on our Theadneedle Street premises expires in two years' time and our Leadenhall Street premises could be subject to a compulsory purchase order in the near future.

5. The 'Investment Plan' envisages that our existing computer will be supplemented with a large new computer to provide management information (as opposed to routine accounting work). Apart from the lack of room, it would be expensive to install the computer in any of our existing offices because of ventilation problems.

6. Although we own the freehold of our Old Broad Street and Throgmorton Avenue premises, there will be a substantial increase in expenses even if we do not expand, as the leases on our Threadneedle and Leadenhall Street premises were signed many years ago and have rentals of £3 and £2 per square foot compared with £6 per square foot being asked on new leases. For our purposes 120 sq. ft. per person is a good approximation to our floor-space needs, excluding the new computer.

7. Unless we can obtain extra accommodation, the growth envisaged in the Corporate Plan cannot take place. Unless we can move some or all of our activities out of Central London we face a major increase in accommodation costs.

> B. Fox
> Manager, Office Services Department
> (Date – about a week earlier
> than the covering minute)

Stage 2. A couple of days before the meeting, each student should receive the following memoranda:

Memorandum from N. Lock to Director of Corporate Planning

Nonsuch Assurance Ltd

To the Director of Corporate Planning:
  c.c. Planning Officers (students' names)

Office Accommodation

1. In the course of a lunchtime conversation yesterday I was told that you were considering Mr Fox's suggestion that some or all of our headquarters activities should be moved from Central London.

2. I am most alarmed!

3. It might be possible to move some activities out of Central London – e.g. Industrial Insurance – but not Marine Insurance. Any savings in rent would be more than offset by lost business if we moved more than fifteen minutes' walk from Lloyd's.

4. Mr James of the Portfolio Management Department assured me that he too would regard a move outside the 'square mile' as suicidal.

5. I would much appreciate being kept in touch with any developments regarding office accommodation.

> N. Lock
> Director of Marine Insurance
> (Date)

Memorandum from J. Andrews to Director of Corporate Planning

Nonsuch Assurance Ltd

Director of Corporate Planning
Director of Marine Insurance
Manager, Portfolio Management
Planning Staff (students' names)

Office Accommodation

1. At the recent Board meeting I was most impressed by the arguments in Mr Fox's paper.

2. At present our Central London staff receive a London

weighting of £150 per annum and are pressing for this to be raised to £200. Time-keeping by staff is a disgrace and labour turnover is double that in our provincial offices.

3. We need not, of course, move all our activities out of London.

4. A search through my files shows that while some employees commute into London Bridge, Cannon Street, Waterloo and Moorgate stations, most use Liverpool Street, Broad Street and Fenchurch Street stations. About a quarter of our staff could travel to Southend without moving house (maximum journey one hour) and about 15 per cent could travel to Romford or Chelmsford.

5. As 85 per cent of our customers are in the South-east and Midlands, I would be surprised if we found a move to a development area worthwhile.

6. So long as we move into existing accommodation and do not buy or lease new offices, the Government's office location policy does not restrict the options open to us. However, if we envisage creating new office accommodation we shall have to justify our location decision in order to obtain an office development permit.

J. Andrews
Director of Personnel
(Date)

Stage 3. The first meeting of the working party is chaired by the teacher in his role of Director of Corporate Planning. While allowing students scope to develop their ideas, his opening comments should focus attention on:

> Why is the firm thinking about its office location policy?
> What are the options open to the firm?
> Are there any constraints which make it pointless pursuing some options?
> Are there any significant advantages from integrating activities within one office rather than splitting them between geographically separate premises?

Towards the end of the meeting, attention should have focused on about three options, e.g. integration of all head office activities within one large Central London office, a total move to a suburban or regional location and a partial move.

Stage 4. At the end of the first meeting of the working party, the students should be divided into three project teams of four members. Each project team should be asked to investigate an option – e.g. a partial move – and complete a report for circulation to the remainder of the working party *before* its next meeting.

Within each project team it is important to ensure that each student has a specific role. For example, one student might investigate the impact of the Government's office location policy on the option concerned, one the cost and availability of office accommodation, one the labour-cost aspects of the option (this might also include consideration of redundancy compensation, retraining, etc.) and one should act as chairman. The chairman is responsible (with or without the assistance of a secretary) for drafting and circulating the team's report and ensuring that any considerations not covered by the proposed division of labour are not forgotten. At this stage, it is important to have supplementary reading material available to be referred to by the project teams as required.

Project teams may complete their work unsupervised or a teaching period may be used. Reports should be brief and be circulated to all participants before the next (final) meeting of the working party.

Stage 5. The last (second) meeting of the working party should discuss the three options and select two to be placed before the Board.

PROBLEMS OF APPLICATION

The printing and distribution of working group reports in between the two meetings of the full working party requires access to duplicating facilities. To prevent the exercise becoming a managerial case study, the teacher should stress the relevance of economic concepts to location decisions. Our warning about the dangers of digressions applies particularly to this case.

VARIANTS

The case can be adapted to many teaching situations. For example, the memoranda outlined above tend to steer the outcome in favour of a partial move within South-east England, but only slight changes would be needed to leave a wider or narrower range of options. Likewise, the conurbation chosen can easily be changed to find an environment closer to the students' experience – e.g. students in Manchester could examine dispersal from Central Manchester to north-east Cheshire. With small groups, students could each take the role of a specific person in the firm, e.g. Mr Fox, etc.

As the case was intended for use with students on introductory courses, little attention has been paid to the mechanics of the decision-making process, or to more precise analysis of the qualitative and quantitative data available in the publications recommended for use. However, the case can be adapted to meet the needs of more advanced students, or to serve as an integrating study. For example, students on a business studies degree course could each be given roles which require a knowledge of a different academic discipline. In such a case, those designated as economists could calculate the d.c.f. rates of return expected on each option. If this is done, it will be necessary to have access to a wide range of source material.

A useful follow-up would be to discuss the problems of dispersal with somebody from a firm which has moved from Central London, or to visit such a firm if this coincided with other educational objectives.

Sources and References

Moving Your Office (L.O.B., free in limited quantities for educational purposes). Gives a brief description of the advantages and disadvantages of dispersal from Central London. Appendices give typical rents outside London, maps of the development areas and office development control areas and case histories of some firms which have decentralised.

A Wise Move (L.O.B., free as above). A collection of case histories of firms which have decentralised.

Annual Reports (L.O.B.) include comments on current Government office location policy, the state of the office accommodation market and summaries of recent research findings. (The 1968–9 report cost 12½p.)

Offices: A Bibliography (L.O.B., free). Includes many valuable references, particularly for more advanced variants of the case.

CHAPTER TWELVE

A Transport Study: Bus Services in the Nottingham Area – Some Effects of the Boundary System

Sylvia Trench[1]

AIMS

This project aimed to show the extent of the deficiencies of the boundary system of bus licensing in Nottingham. It had a definite practical purpose – to try to give some local publicity to the wastefulness of the present arrangements in the hope that some pressure would be put on the authorities concerned to revise the boundary system locally.

The project was essentially an illustration of the economic consequences of one aspect of the bus-licensing system. At present, bus services are licensed under an Act of 1930 whereby operators are given a degree of monopoly on a specified route. If routes overlap, as in the case where long-distance or suburban services duplicate part of a local city service, the city operator is often protected from competition for local passengers within its boundaries. In some areas bus companies make arrangements to pool revenues over the common section of their route and passengers are free to catch whichever bus comes first. In other areas the long-distance operator may carry local passengers at a minimum fare which is above that of the local service. But in many areas, including Nottingham, the protection takes the form of an absolute prohibition on both picking up and setting down a passenger within the City Transport boundary. Passengers in such areas suffer the inconvenience and irritation of being unable to board a bus going to their destination even when it has stopped beside them. Moreover the revision of the boundary regulations might in many cases make it possible to reduce the number of buses required on a given route and so provide economies of operation.

[1] The author wishes to record that the project was the work of two students, Graham Edwards and Richard Gibson, who designed the case studies and carried out most of the data collection and analysis themselves.

These protection regulations arise from the attempt of the Traffic Commissioners who issue the licences to try to be fair to different operators, and to protect the economic viability of the services provided by each individual operator. The system in each locality has grown up over the last forty years in a piece-meal fashion as cities have grown and routes have been licensed to serve new residential areas. *A priori* reasoning suggests it would be a very unlikely accident if the pattern of routes and picking-up points that grew up in this way was in fact the most rational and economic arrangement of services. On the other hand, the gains from reorganisation might be trivial. The duplication may be necessary to provide long-distance passengers with a through service. Buses might need to carry empty seats over part of their journeys so that long-distance passengers can be picked up at later stages. There seems to have been little detailed examination of the possibilities for co-ordination and improvement.[1] Presumably in the areas where Passenger Transport Authorities have been established under the 1968 Transport Act such studies will be carried out. Outside those areas the formation of the National Bus Company has reduced the number of separate companies involved in providing services and may promote some further examination. In a few areas, however, 'independent' operators remain, and there seems to be no formal machinery for promoting co-ordination.

In any attempt to rationalise services, it would seem sensible to try to determine how they would be provided if there were only one operator. Having done that, then considerations of fairness could, if desired, influence the allocation of revenues between operators. This study aimed to overcome the inertia of those bodies committed to the existing arrangements by attempting to quantify the potential gains from reorganisation to both passengers and operators and to show that they might well be substantial. It was clearly not a blueprint for reorganisation but a very inexpensive study whicn, at the least, established a case for a modest expenditure on more comprehensive research into the possibilities of boundary revision.

[1] A study of the operation of the boundary system in Leicester by Clifford Sharp, *Problems of Urban Passenger Transport* (Leicester University Press, 1967) is a notable exception which gave two Nottingham University students the idea of doing a similar study in Nottingham and at the same time going on to develop a simple cost–benefit analysis of some selected revisions.

Since it involved costing alternative bus services and estimating the benefits of rearranging their routes and pick-up points, the case gave the students experience both in manipulating costings for bus services and in an economic valuation of benefits to passengers.

LEVEL AND REQUIREMENTS

The two students who undertook the project were third-year honours students taking an option in the economics of transport. It also happened that the students who asked to do this project had both taken a particular interest in bus operations and had an understanding of bus scheduling and operating problems well above that of the average 'layman'. This knowledge was probably very valuable in two ways: first, they selected routes for their case studies which proved to be excellent illustrations of the point; second, they were able to make a little survey data go a long way. Since they could only do a limited amount of actual seat and passenger counts they were able to make good choices of when and where to carry these out. The students used some of their own time for collecting data, and we spent £2 on paying other students for assistance with a bigger count during a peak period.

NECESSARY PREPARATORY WORK

This is difficult to separate from the exercise itself. The students collected their data over one and a half terms in small bursts of activity, as a course project. Only after their final examinations did we get a chance to sit down and carefully consider how to calculate the economic assessment and what crude assumptions could reasonably be made to cover gaps in these data. The preparatory work is therefore hard to isolate; probably it is fairest to say that the preparatory stage consisted of finding two 'cases' relevant to the point they were trying to illustrate. Graham Edwards took one particular service to an isolated estate, which he felt on the basis of intuition and map reading could be better served by the city operator. Richard Gibson calculated the proportion of long-distance buses on each main road at various times of the day and selected two roads on which there was both a large number of services and a (slight) majority

113

of long-distance buses. In such circumstances it seemed possible that local buses might be superfluous for much of the day if out-of-town operators were permitted to pick up and set down passengers without restriction. Having selected two routes, the students then worked out where and when they would collect suitable data and stood at the principal city centre bus stops and outer terminals to count passengers on the buses.

It was both necessary and desirable to consult the bus companies concerned; clearly they might have given useful advice on whether they had previously considered any route reorganisations of the kind; they might have had some data on the number of empty seats at key points on the journey; they could have had and might have divulged some information on their particular operating costs. As it happened, the bus companies concerned either ignored our letters or declined to give any information. This was not surprising, since the study was testing a possible reorganisation which would involve extra organisational effort and would disturb the existing financial *status quo* between operators.

THE CASE STUDIES

We looked at two of the many possible ways in which services might be improved if we took the hypothetical single-operator approach and ignored the probability that changing bus schedules would benefit one operator at another's expense. The first study examined the possibility of abolishing two routes serving a particular estate, and instead serving the area by extending some existing services. In this case passengers who might have lost by the diversion would be compensated by allowing long-distance services to pick up and set down within the city boundary. The second study looked at a group of routes served by both long-distance and city buses within the city boundary, to see whether any city bus services would be superfluous if long-distance services could pick up and set down within the boundary.

I. *Extending the City Service*

The Rylands is a residential and industrial estate about five miles from the centre of Nottingham. It is outside the boundary of the area served by Nottingham City Transport (N.C.T.) which was established following the 1930 Act, and is served exclusively by two stage services run by an independent operator, Barton Transport Ltd. These services link the estate with Beeston, a local shoping centre, and with the centre of Nottingham. Buses on these routes, Nos. 1A and 29, are not allowed to pick up passengers going into Nottingham inside the City Transport boundary. On journeys out of Nottingham they may pick up passengers at N.C.T. stops but the passengers may not alight until they are outside the boundary. The service to those who live or work on the estate is not very frequent. In the morning peak period (7.15–9.15) there are two buses an hour on each service and throughout the rest of the day there is one bus per hour on each. In the evening peak (16.30–18.30) there are two buses an hour leaving the City. The capacity of these buses varies between 41 and 70 according to the time of day.

The total number of journeys made by these buses each day (Sunday to Friday)[1] is shown in Table 12.1.

TABLE 12.1

Service:	1A	29
IN per day	21	17
OUT per day	19	15
Total both services	72	

Moreover, there is a lot of unused capacity even during the peak periods. Counts were taken on one day[2] of empty seats on buses leaving the estate.

TABLE 12.2

Route	Time	No. of buses	Total capacity	No. of empty seats	
1A	7.15–9.15	4	180	45	61*
1A	11.00–12.00	1	41	30	34*
29	7.15–9.15	3	139	68	
29	11.00–12.00	1	49	40	

* Spare capacity on 1A after Beeston Square.

[1] Frequency is increased slightly on Saturdays.
[2] Tuesday, 4 February 1969. A Tuesday was chosen as a weekday without any special features like early closing or weekend shopping. For traffic surveys it is normally found that Tuesday multiplied by five gives fairly reliable estimates of weekday traffic.

The figures on the 1A after Beeston Square are given to show the number of passengers travelling from the Rylands just to the Square – the local shopping centre.

These figures show that there is a considerable amount of spare capacity on these routes – 28 per cent of total capacity during the peak period of the day analysed.

About two miles from the estate, the more important shopping/residential area of Beeston is well served by N.C.T. services into the city. It is also on the route into the city of a large number of Barton's long-distance buses which pass through but must not pick up and set down passengers whose journeys both begin and end within the boundary. Thus N.C.T. run three services from Beeston into Nottingham via University Boulevard: the 4, 4A and 5A. Barton's run twelve different routes which run along University Boulevard: 3, 3A, 3B, 3C, 5A, 5B, 5X, 10, 11, 32, 33 and 40. Fig. 12.1 shows the routes of these buses.

In order to estimate the requirements of a new service combining the N.C.T. and Barton's routes, it was first necessary to estimate the total amount of traffic using all the present services along University Boulevard that terminate in Beeston. This yields the requirements of a hypothetical service. The traffic was estimated by counting the numbers of passengers leaving

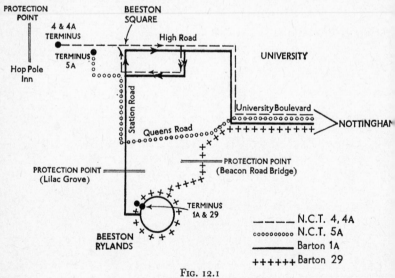

Fig. 12.1

the City at midday and during the evening peak. These figures are given in the following table:[1]

TABLE 12.3

Route	Time	No. of buses	Total capacity	No. of passengers
1A	11.00–12.00	1	41	5
29	,,	1	56	6
4	,,	3	228	60
4A	,,	3	228	55
5A	,,	3	228	21
1A	16.30–18.30	2	82	38
29	,,	2	108	46
4	,,	6+ 2 extras	577	299
4A	,,	6	456	261
5A	,,	6	456	177

This traffic census suggests that a different service, yielding benefits to both passengers and operators, could be provided by adopting the following proposals:

1. Discontinue the present 1A and 29 services.
2. Replace these by the N.C.T. services 4, 4A and 5A re-routed to start from the Rylands at the terminus of the 1A and 29. The 4 and 4A would then go to Beeston Square and on to the City and the 5A, which follows a different route, to Queens Road and on to the City.

Thus in both cases these N.C.T. services will fail to pick up a few of their passengers who join the buses at their original terminus, but continue to follow their original route over the more heavily loaded sector from the centre of Beeston into Nottingham. The Rylands passengers have a more frequent service but are carried over a slightly more circuitous route.

The counts of empty seats showed that the re-routed N.C.T. services would have adequate capacity even at peak periods to replace the Barton's services. The following figures are based on Table 12.3 and are illustrated on Fig. 12.2.

[1] The figures for N.C.T. were taken on 4 February and for Barton's on the following Tuesday. Tuesdays were chosen for the reasons given in fn. 2 on p. 115.

E

Total capacity of hypothetical services in the
  peak (i.e. the present 4, 4A, 5A)   1489
Total number of passengers now travelling
  to Beeston and the Rylands   821

Thus, even if the one-day count taken was not representative
of peak load,[1] there is still sufficient capacity to accommodate
an increase.

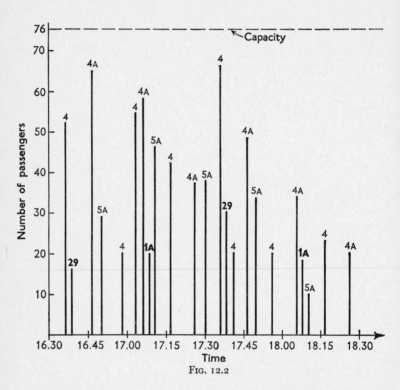

Fig. 12.2

One further route adjustment serves to compensate the small
number of passengers who have suffered from moving the terminus of the N.C.T. 4, 4A and 5A services. Since these termini
are on the route of the Barton's services listed on p. 116, it is only
necessary to move the City Transport boundary inward less
than half a mile to Beeston Square so that these passengers
may use any of the twelve routes passing by. This measure
would also give Barton's, the operator, who lost revenue from

[1] Further samples taken suggest that the load does not vary considerably.
118

discontinuing the Rylands service, some compensating revenue
on other services. Whether the compensation was adequate
could be examined afterwards.

Having examined the technical feasibility of the proposals,
it is then necessary to evaluate the benefits and costs. In general
it appears that both passengers and operators gain. Passengers
from the Rylands have a more frequent service offset by a
slightly slower journey. Bus operators save 72 daily runs. The
fare levels at present charged differ only by 1*d*.[1]

The main points of comparison are summarised in the following tables:

TABLE 12.4

Present service for Rylands passengers	*Hypothetical service*
38 inward buses	141 inward buses
34 outward buses	142 outward buses
Quick journeys on unfilled buses	Slightly slower journeys, but higher capacity utilisation
Fare 1*s*. 1*d*.	Fare 1*s*. 1*d*.
Time to City 17 mins.	Time to City 22 mins.

Since Rylands passengers both gained in frequency but lost
in journey time, it was necessary to try and evaluate the net
time gained or lost. In order to present an overall economic
estimate of the gain from the proposals, the time savings would
also need to be valued as a social gain in addition to the more
tangible savings in operating costs. The evaluation used is shown
in Table 12.5.

We made a crude simple assumption about waiting time –
that passengers arriving at random would wait an average of
half the service frequency, and that passengers who 'timed'
their arrival would be roughly balanced by those just missing a
bus and waiting the full service interval. On a residential estate
this assumption probably overstates the waiting time under the
old infrequent service, since passengers are probably in a good
position to time their arrival. This probably does not apply to
their journeys from the city centre. Since the time savings
values are such a small part of total benefits, the lack of sophis-

---

[1] All money values in these two case studies are expressed in old currency
units, as the study took place before decimalisation.

TABLE 12.5

Evaluation of time savings to Rylands passengers

Present frequency	30 mins.	Implied average waiting time	15 mins.
		Journey time	17 mins.
		Total	32 mins.
New frequency	6 mins.	Implied average waiting time	3 mins.
		Journey time	22 mins.
		Total	25 mins.

Time saving of new service: 7 minutes per passenger.

tication here was not important. Had the students had more time it might have been useful to have carried out some counts of the numbers of passengers actually waiting at stops and the time spent. But it clearly necessary to give the increased frequency a positive valuation – passengers will, other things being equal, always prefer a more frequent to a less frequent service.

Having estimated the amount of time savings we then gave them a money value. The hourly rate at which to value non-working time is a subject of some controversy among economists engaged in cost–benefit analysis. We decided to avoid presenting a complicated paper with alternative valuations, and settled for the minimum figure and the one then commonly used by the Ministry of Transport and valued it at 3s. per hour. This gave a money value to the time saving per passenger per trip of 4·2d. The aggregate amount of time saved on these routes and consequently the aggregate money value are difficult to estimate since the study was not sufficiently broad to provide a reliable estimate of total passengers on these routes. However, in order to give some idea of the magnitude of the savings to be made, we have used the minimum figures from our one-day survey.

Passengers no longer served by N.C.T. services after the terminus points were moved but allowed to board the long-distance

TABLE 12.6

Estimated number of passengers
using 1A and 29 on day of sample   607

Aggregate time savings of
  hypothetical service at 7
  minutes per passenger

$$607 \times 7 = 4249 \text{ minutes}$$
$$= 70\cdot8 \text{ hours per day}$$
$$= 354 \text{ hours per week*}$$
$$= 18,408 \text{ hours per year.}$$

Money value of 18,408 hours at
  3s. per hour $= £2761.$

* Assuming a five-day week.

buses passing by would have a reduction of average waiting time of $2\frac{1}{2}$ minutes and a reduction in journey time of 7 minutes – a benefit of 5·1d. by the same criterion. No survey of the numbers involved here was taken, but assuming the number transferring to be a minimum of 5 per service,[1] a minimum value for the savings could be calculated from the number of time-tabled buses as follows:

No. of passengers   1000

Aggregate time saving   7000 minutes $= 116\cdot6$ hours per day
                                     $= 30,334$ hours per year

Money value of 30,334 hours at
  3s. per hour $= £4550.$

Evaluation of Cost Savings to Operators from Discontinuance of 1A and 29

Savings would accrue from the following items:

Labour costs, fuel and oil, depreciation, servicing, tyres, administration.

The present Barton's services probably cost roughly as follows:

         Route 1A   £12,000 per annum.
         Route 29   £11,000 per annum.

The extension of the City service would probably add about £1500 per annum to current costs. These costings were not

[1] This is a very low estimate, especially during the peak.

given by the bus companies but were calculated from published data on bus costs, applied to the mileages and timetabled frequencies of the service. Details of the basis of the bus cost calculations are given in Table 12.8. Thus there would appear to be potential savings of at least £20,000 per annum plus time savings to passengers worth over £7000 per annum.

II. *Long-distance or Local Buses on a Group of Routes*

In this study, we wanted to discover the number of empty seats on long-distance services which might be occupied by local passengers if they too could be carried. On some roads, such as those to Arnold and Mapperley, long-distance services account for a very small proportion of all buses, and hence their contribution to carrying local passengers could be only small. On several other roads, however, there are more long-distance than local buses, and it was two of these instances – Derby Road and University Boulevard routes – which we studied. We took small samples both during the peak and off-peak periods of the number of passengers on both local and long-distance services on these roads, and found that only during two short periods during the evening peak was the number of spare seats on long-distance services less than the number of local passengers departing Nottingham during the same ten-minute period (see Table 12.8). This would suggest that, with the exception of the 'peak-within-the-peak', there would be no need for local buses on these routes if long-distance buses were allowed to carry the passengers.

Counts were taken of spare seats available on long-distance buses leaving the City terminus whose routes would be a satisfactory substitute for passengers on local services. Counts were also taken at the same times of passengers on the relevant N.C.T. services. We did not have the resources to count passengers boarding buses between the terminus and the City boundary on all these buses. Sample checks of passengers joining buses en route out of the City suggested that a suitable allowance would be 10–15 per cent. Thus the table below shows the numbers counted at the terminus with a 12½ per cent addition to N.C.T. passengers and a 12½ per cent deduction from the number of empty seats observed on long-distance buses.

TABLE 12.7

Comparison of supply of empty seats on long-distance buses with the demand for seats by local passengers

Time period	Passengers on N.C.T. services	Empty seats on long-distance buses
Derby Road		
16.30–16.40	115	108
16.41–16.50	39	92
16.51–17.00	57	50
17.01–17.10	82	81
17.11–17.20	47	72
17.21–17.30	60	13
17.31–17.40	80	57
17.41–17.50	27	157
17.51–18.00	27	48
18.01–18.10	21	111
18.11–18.20	0	50
University Boulevard		
16.30–16.40	83	92
16.41–16.50	105	78
16.51–17.00	22	31
17.01–17.10	179	73
17.11–17.20	47	138
17.21–17.30	83	16
17.31–17.40	77	66
17.41–17.50	115	63
17.51–18.00	22	59
18.01–18.10	49	89
18.11–18.20	22	113

If local N.C.T. services on these routes were curtailed to operate only at peak periods and all day on Saturday, very considerable savings could be made. At present the routes which we studied appear to cost something over £150,000 per annum.[1] The service which we have described here would probably cost not more than £60,000 per annum.[2] Thus there appear to

[1] Estimated from timetables and cost data in Table 12.7.
[2] If split shifts of a total of four hours in twelve were paid as if they were eight-hour shifts, the cost would be less than £50,000 per annum. Staff might, of course, be unwilling to work such shifts.

be cost savings worth about £90,000 per annum (gross) by considering this approach. On the other hand, journey times for long-distance passengers would be increased, partly by more frequent stops for local passengers, and partly through small diversions which would be necessary to cover those local routes served only by local buses. However, the value of this increase in time is probably not more than about £8000 per annum,[1] and increased fuel costs are unlikely to be greater than a further £1000–£2000 per annum. Hence there is likely to be a net saving of at least £80,000 per annum.

These calculations can give no more than the most general idea of the savings which might be achieved, since they are based on a small sample, and on general estimates of operating costs (since bus operators' actual costs were not available). They do, however, seem to indicate the probable existence of alternative, more economical ways of operating bus services, if the distortions of the licensing system and protection areas were removed.

TABLE 12.8

The basis of calculation of cost savings in operation

The following figures were used in the calculation:

Labour	20s. per crew per hour
	(14s. per driver-conductor per hour)
Cleaning and	3s. 6d. per hour of operation *plus*
maintenance	20s. per day used
Fuel and oil	7·2d. per mile
Insurance and licence	20s. per day used *plus* 1·75d. per mile
Depreciation	20s. per day
Tyres	1d. per mile

(Administration is assumed to be approximately 23s. per vehicle per day but was not included in these calculations.) These figures are based on information in *Pay and Conditions of Busmen*, National Board for Prices and Incomes, Report No. 16, Cmnd 3012 (May 1966), and K. M. Gwilliam, *Transport and Public Policy* (London, 1964).

[1] Assumes 100 passengers per hour travelling on these routes and subject to about 6 minutes increase in time which is valued at 3s. per hour.

This project required some knowledge of bus operations and some facility with timetables. A full-scale survey was out of the question within the time scale of a course project with very little in the way of extra assistance. Since its object was only to draw attention to the order of magnitude of potential savings, it seemed reasonable to gross up very small samples taken at reasonably representative times. Even so a lot of the data required supplementing with timetable analysis and odd sample counts to see if crude assumptions were not unreasonable. As we put the paper together it became apparent that we had not done any counts of some factors relevant to potential benefits (for example, the passengers boarding at the original 4 and 4A terminus in the Rylands study). We had then to make do with 'minimum' estimates that no one could reasonably question, and therefore probably understated the case.

The only other difficulty was the non cooperation of the bus companies, whose reluctance to supply data is understandable. It should be noted, however, that response to the final paper circulated to bus companies and other interested parties was generally favourable.

VARIANTS

It would seem a useful exercise to repeat in any locality where conditions exist similar to these outlined here, namely a boundary system enforced by prohibition rather than fare- or revenue-pooling arrangements. It would be important to have one member of the group who is really familiar with the geography and scheduling of bus services. It would be possible to collect data much more fully if larger numbers of students were participating and could travel on a sufficient number of buses to count passengers boarding at different points. However, the value of the project in this case does not seem to have been diminished by the size of the samples taken. Moreover the students benefited more from discussing the problems of how to handle their data than from the chore of collecting it. Thus a project with a larger group would only be of value if they were all genuinely involved in these discussions.

CHAPTER THIRTEEN

A Cost–Benefit Study of a Railway Closure

Sylvia Trench[1]

AIMS

This was a study of a railway line running from Nottingham north through Mansfield to Worksop and serving an area with a population of between 150,000 and 200,000. Passenger services had been withdrawn in 1964 when the line was said to be losing around £150,000 per annum. These losses were estimated on the basis of what are now regarded as inappropriately excessive methods of working for this kind of route – steam traction and fully-staffed stations. Local authorities in the area had unsuccessfully opposed the closure at the time. Subsequently, when government policy seemed to be more sympathetic to unremunerative railway services and the possibility of subsidies was being considered, the local authorities formed a committee to campaign for its reopening. They approached Nottingham University for help in producing an assessment of the economic prospects and social benefits of the line.

A grant of £200 was made available to finance a small study within the Department of Industrial Economics. It seemed that the best way to use the funds would be to employ some of our own students who were looking for a vacation job. Those who offered were largely second- and third-year economics students who were taking or intended to take the economics of transport as a third-year option. This study was never consciously undertaken as a course project, but as we worked it became apparent that it was serving a very useful teaching purpose. It was almost a course in transport economics in microcosm. It involved some practical exercise in a great many of the prob-

[1] Thanks are due to the students who worked on this study: Richard Gibson for an extensive analysis of bus services and a major role in organising the bus survey; Gordon Craig for background research and for doing most of the laborious calculations; and Fleur Rees, Ingrid Jacobsen and Michael Whither for undertaking sections of the research and survey analysis.

lems which would normally form part of a transport economics course. For example, we had to assess the likely profit or loss of a reopened service. Since the service had been withdrawn several years ago, and was badly run down in the period before that, there were no usable figures of passenger traffic from which to estimate revenues. It was necessary to proceed as though for a completely new service and consider the possibilities of traffic generation, car-to-rail diversion and, most importantly, the degree to which rail might be a preferable substitute to bus services for individual journeys. Then in order to provide a financial assessment we needed to cost the service. Again, past data were not available since the previous service had used steam traction and fully staffed stations. A new service, if it could be justified at all, would have to be run at minimum cost using diesel multiple units, conductor guards collecting fares and unstaffed halts. Thus we had to cost the service from scratch on the basis of what was known about costs under such conditions. This was an interesting exercise in costing a very simple passenger service. We also needed to see whether future developments in the area, residential and industrial, were likely to increase or decrease potential traffic and whether they would provide any sort of regional or social support for reopening the service. The possibility of support for the case from its contribution to relieving traffic congestion had to be investigated and evaluated. Thus we had to examine local origin and destination surveys to see what car traffic was passing on our routes. Finally we had to evaluate time savings to potential passengers and assess any other social benefits.

The study therefore gave the students who helped an insight into the complexity of an apparently simple problem and some experience in handling very different kinds of data. In the early stages the different topics could be parcelled out to individual students who prepared their own reports. Altogether five students undertook substantial pieces of work on the project and it could easily have involved up to eight or nine each doing independent parts of the study.

Level and Requirements

The students were second- and third-year honours students. Most of them had not yet done any transport economics. The major part of the exercise called for a fairly extensive survey of bus passengers for which we employed 32 paid students. Some were employed for a pilot exercise and all took part in a one-day full-scale survey. The cost of these surveys was £120. Processing the data on to punched cards and sorting them took about one week's work shared between two students who were inexperienced when they began. We also required the use of punched-card sorting equipment.

The survey costs were almost entirely for labour and travelling. A very simple interview form was needed so that stationery costs were trivial and interviewers worked with a cardboard backing and a bulldog clip. Recruiting, briefing, scheduling and transporting interviewers was very laborious and would have been very difficult if we had not been recruiting within our own student body. Moreover interviewers were working in relatively lonely places as early as 5 a.m. and as late as midnight. Clearly such interviewers would need to be relatively mature and resilient.

Necessary Preparatory Work

A number of the exercises outlined at the beginning of this chapter were carried out as preparatory work and not taken any further into the main study since they appeared to show nothing worthy of more thorough investigation. They will therefore be detailed here.

An examination of future plans for development provided a self-contained exercise for one student who interviewed local planning officers and important employers in the area and prepared a separate paper on her findings. At the time of the study (1968) the Regional Council had not formulated any plans, and she found that such proposals as were then being aired were unlikely to lead to any generation of traffic along the rail route.

The same student carried out a study of works transport in the area. This was another self-contained exercise. Important employers in Nottingham were interviewed about the extent to which they provided special bus services on the route and on their interest in drawing in labour from population centres like Mansfield and Kirkby. The results were interesting: one company was found to be running five different services between the Worksop district and Nottingham more or less along the route and taking largely female workers direct to their factory. We felt this was a good reflection of the inadequacy of existing services, and of the degree to which employers of female labour were needing to draw on labour reserves north of Nottingham. However, the company felt their bus services would be required even if the rail service were reopened, so we did not adjust any of our survey calculations. Other employers were more sceptical about actively seeking to attract long-distance commuters. Clearly improved transport services would extend the labour market for growing industries, but the factor would have to be left as an intangible and unquantifiable benefit which would not be part of the substantive case for reopening the service.

Another separate exercise was to examine road traffic into Nottingham from the area of the railway line. Another student took this as a self-contained exercise and examined a recent origin and destination survey carried out by Nottingham Corporation. He also examined Nottingham's highway plan to see if any expensive projects could reasonably be allocated any incremental cost due to congestion caused by car traffic along the route of the railway line. In neither case did he find any evidence that merited further study or calculations.

We examined data from the Journey to Work tables of the 1966 Census. An analysis of these was useful in selecting the points on the line between which there was significant journey-to-work travel, and it helped us to eliminate a number of possible interview points on the passenger surveys which would have produced little of value.

We also looked at the possibility of applying gravity models to predict the likely flow between major points on our routes. These might have served as a check on the reliability of other data. We decided that they were too generalised for our purpose; moreover our prime concern was with the model split between bus and rail and only a survey could adequately cover the particular peculiarities of competing bus and rail routes in this case.

It was decided to estimate potential traffic for the hypothetical rail service by finding out how many passengers would derive faster and more convenient journeys from it, and assuming that those who would derive a clear benefit would transfer to rail. We did not think an interview approach on the lines 'Would you use the line if . . .' would give reliable results.

Further, we were dealing with a geographical area 28 miles long with a population of 150,000 to 200,000 of which not more than 10,000 were likely to be even potential rail passengers. A sample survey based on residence or place of work would need to be very large to be sure of finding even a small proportion of the group whose journeys were relevant to our study. We had to concentrate our surveys very precisely at the points where potential travellers would be moving.

Thus there was a large amount of preparatory work required to map all bus routes any sections of which linked any two stations on the line. We then eliminated a number of possible rail journeys between points on the route where bus services provided faster journeys. Bus timetables were compared with the timings of a hypothetical rail service.[1]

We also visited the sites of the disused passenger stations to see how far they were from the main shopping and residential centres. Those which were badly placed and could expect to attract very few passengers were eliminated from the survey. For the others, we identified nearby bus stops at which to position interviewers.

We designed a questionnaire on which interviewers could quickly record the replies of a number of passengers as they boarded their buses (see p. 132). Its most important question was 'Where are you going to get off this bus?' Passengers who mentioned a destination off the railway route would be quickly eliminated. Those who mentioned a centre on the route were then asked if they were going to a particular place, pre-selected as nearest to the railway station. If they said 'yes' they were recorded as a potential passenger. Those replying 'no' were asked if their destination was near this point, in which case they were so recorded and scaled down by half in the tabulations. The assumption here was that a random sample would contain as many passengers beginning their journey nearer the station than the bus stop as farther from it. 'Near' was left deliberately subjective – interviewers asked to define it were told to say 'about five to ten minutes' walk' – since it was passengers' attitude to the distance rather than its exact mileage which would determine whether they would walk to the station to

[1] The hypothetical service was timed using British Rail timetables for routes where distances and station intervals were comparable with those on our service.

save time on their journey.[1] The questionnaire was tested by a pilot survey and proved workable and easy to use at speed.

Interviewers needed a detailed briefing. They had to understand why it was important to be accurate about the exact point of leaving the bus. They also needed to know enough about the geography of the rail route and its relation to bus stops to interpret passengers' replies quickly.

THE CASE STUDY

The main part of the study was an exercise to assess whether British Rail would make a loss if they reopened passenger services on this route. The possible extent of social benefits was subsidiary and secondary, since even if they were to prove substantial the problem remained of who would pay for them and how they would be financed. This particular route did not qualify for any of the grants from the central Government available under the 1968 Transport Act, and the only possible source of subsidy finance would be from the local authorities themselves. Clearly the financial expectations would be central to both a commercial or a subsidy decision, since a subsidy cost would need to be set against the benefits.

The most difficult part of the study was the survey designed to identify potential passengers for a reopened rail service. The preparatory work has already been explained. It enabled us to narrow down seven key interview points on the route at which we would find nearly all the passengers whose journeys would be faster by rail.[2] The student interviewers covered these points in shifts from the time of the first bus (around 5 a.m.) until the last bus left (between 11 and 12 p.m.).

In the extreme north of the area (between Shirebrook and Worksop) the bus service was so infrequent that interviews

---

[1] Questions 2–7 on the questionnaire look complicated. In fact they were designed to pick up accurately passenger flows involving an interchange, and the key information only required recording on the original list of destinations by a single letter. Further questions were only used if there was time and provided some supplementary data on rail interchange, sex, luggage and number of children.

[2] Although our route was crossed by over forty possible bus routes, flows from south of Mansfield to destinations northwards required an interchange at Mansfield and passengers could be interviewed at their interchange point.

ORIGIN............... TIME................ CODE................ BUS NO............... INTV...............

' I am working on a survey of the effects of closing the railway line between Nottingham, Mansfield, and Worksop. Would you mind telling me something about your journey?'

' Where are you going to get off this bus?' TICK THE PLACE BELOW IF THE JOURNEY IS TO THAT EXACT PLACE. IF NOT, BUT IF A TOWN LISTED BELOW IS MENTIONED, ASK *' Is it near . . . ?'* (NEAR IS 5–10 MINS. WALK) AND IF IT IS NEAR THE PLACE MARK *' X'*. TICK *' Other'* IF IT IS NOT AT OR NEAR A PLACE LISTED BELOW.

1. NOTTM. Huntingdon/Mount St.													
2. RADFORD, Marsh, Faraday/ Triumph Rd.													
3. BULWELL Market													
4. HUCKNALL Market/Byron/ Station Rd.													
5. LINBY Lane													
6. NEWSTEAD Village/Annesley Coll.													
7. KIRKBY, Nags Head/Level Crossing													
8. SUTTON Portland Square													
9. MANSFIELD West Gate/Stockwell Gate													
10. (MANSFIELD) WOODHOUSE													
11. SHIREBROOK Market Place													
12. LANGWITH North St. (not L. Junc.)													
13. CRESWELL Elmfields/Regors Cin.													
14. WHITWELL Square/Boot & Shoe													
15. WORKSOP Bus station													
16. OTHER													

IF *' Other'* END THE INTERVIEW, YOU NEED NOT RECORD ANYTHING ELSE.

2. *Is that your final destination?*

YES													
NO													

IF *' Yes'* PASS ON TO QUESTION 5. IF *' No'* ASK

3. *How will you reach your final destination?*

TICK													
BUS													
TRAIN													
CAR/TAXI													
FOOT/OTHER													

IF *' Bus'* ASK QUESTION 4. ALL OTHERS GO ON TO QUESTION 5.

132

4. *When you change on to the other bus where will you get off that bus?* MARK 'F' IN THE COLUMNS FOR QUESTION I IF THE PLACE IS AT OR NEAR ONE OF THE PLACES LISTED OR MARK 'F' BY '*Other*'.

5. *Did your journey begin here?*

TICK	YES														
	NO														

IF '*Yes*' PASS ON TO QUESTION 8. IF '*No*' ASK QUESTION 6.

6. *How did you come here?*

TICK	BUS									
	CAR/TAXI									
	TRAIN									
	FOOT/OTHER									

IF '*Bus*' ASK QUESTION 7. ALL OTHERS GO ON TO QUESTION 8.

7. *Where did you get on the bus which brought you here?* MARK 'O' IN THE COLUMNS FOR QUESTION I IF THE PLACE IS AT OR NEAR ONE OF THE PLACES ON THE LIST. IF NOT MARK 'O' BY '*Other*'.

8. *What is the purpose of your journey?*

TICK	WORK									
	SHOPPING									
	EDUCATION									
	ENTERTAINMENT									
	HEALTH									
	OTHER									

TO BE COMPLETED BY THE INTERVIEWER:

9. TICK TO RECORD A PASSENGER WHOSE INTERVIEW IS KNOWN IN ADVANCE TO BE IDENTICAL TO THAT IN ADJACENT LEFT COLUMN AND DRAW A LINE UP TO OCCUPY COLUMN.

	TICK									
10. TICK WHETHER MALE OVER 14 ...										
FEMALE OVER 14										
CHILD 3–14 YRS.										
11. TICK IF PASSENGER HAS CHILD UNDER 3										
TICK ACCOMPANIED BY LUGGAGE/PUSHCHAIR										

12. TICK UNRECORDED BOARDERS

No. of
TICKS

133

were not practical. Instead observers rode on two of the five daily buses noting on a chart passengers whose origins and destinations were both at possible transfer points on the railway route.[1] As we were unable to cover all five buses, we multiplied our results by $\frac{5}{2}$ and assumed that the two buses ridden would be typical of all five. Since these assumptions involved a high possibility of error, we presented the financial results for this part of the route separately.

The sample survey taken in this way covered a very high proportion of potential passengers. In fact this was almost a complete enumeration for one day in the year except where passengers refused to answer or were boarding the buses in such large numbers that there was not time to interview them all. Interviewers counted the number of 'uninterviewed boarders' and these were later allocated to flows on the route in the same proportion as boarders interviewed at the same stop. We interviewed a total of 5200 passengers and recorded 3800 additional boarders; thus our interview sample for the day was 58 per cent. We carried out the survey on a Tuesday in April on the advice of experienced transport consultants that Tuesday is a good average day without special features and that Tuesday multiplied by five normally gives a reliable estimate for weekday traffic. Since April is again a month without special seasonal peculiarities, we thought our weekday estimate multiplied by 52 would give a reasonable annual estimate for weekday traffic.[2] We made no attempt to calculate the Saturday traffic. This would have been markedly different. Another survey would have doubled the cost and acquired data for one day only. Bus companies were not able to supply figures showing different loadings for weekdays and Saturdays on their bus routes so we could not even adjust our weekday data. We therefore based our final financial estimates on five days' revenue plus alternative assumptions for Saturdays: that it was a quarter, a half, or equal to weekday flows. Sundays were

[1] This is not difficult if the observer carries a prepared chart of the layout of the bus and has learnt in advance the number code of relevant origins and destinations.

[2] As it happened we had freak snowstorms and blizzards on the survey day. We were not able to allow for this but noted that our survey probably understated the flows of shopping and leisure journeys which might have been affected.

excluded both from revenue and cost estimates. The case for reopening would need to stand or fall on its weekday earnings, and Sunday traffics are normally so low that they will not make any contribution to the overheads of the service.

The survey covered flows in one direction only. This effectively halved the cost of surveying the routes in question. We interviewed only those boarding buses and stationed interviewers where they would pick up passengers going in one direction only. This seems a reasonable procedure, since most people travelling in one direction will return on the same day and a random sample should pick up as many one-way journeys as it misses one-way journeys in the reverse direction. The flows recorded by the survey were therefore doubled to give the daily flows in both directions.

Table 13.1 shows the estimated number of passenger jouneys in a week potentially transferable to rail as estimated by the survey.

Notes to Table 13.1

Where flows have been marked ×, our interviewers were in a position to record travellers making such journeys, but none was recorded on the survey date. We were not in a position to record journeys for flows where the box is left blank. For some flows our interviewers were positioned to pick up all but one or two bus routes covering the flow (the figure is marked † to indicate a small degree of underestimation). In cases where our interviewers were not positioned to record all the important buses carrying the flow, the figure has been marked ‡ to indicate significant underestimation. There is therefore some degree of underestimation in the figures in Table 13.1.

Taking these passenger estimates, potential weekly revenue has been calculated using half the bus return fare as the possible railway charge. This seemed a more appropriate rate to use than basing estimates on different standard mileage charges, since the railways would be unwise to use a standard fare if it were higher than that of a competing bus service, except where they have a substantial time advantage. On the other hand, in trying to make a service pay they would be undercharging in relation to market conditions if they priced below it. If an actual

TABLE 13·1

Estimated number of passenger journeys per week (excluding Saturdays) potentially transferable to rail

To \ From	Nottingham Midland 01	Radford 02	Bulwell Market 03	Hucknall Byron 04	Linby 05	Newstead West 06	Kirkby in Ashfield 07	Sutton Junction 08	Mansfield Town 09	Mansfield Woodhouse 10	Shirebrook West 11	Langwith 12	Elmton and Cresswell 13	Whitwell 14
Radford 02	100													
Bulwell Market 03	5910	50												
Hucknall Byron 04	160†	10	60											
Linby 05	350	X	30	700										
Newstead West 06	1195	10	80	240	200									
Kirkby in Ashfield 07	765	X	X	140†	20	940								
Sutton Junction 08	401	X	X	X	50†	30	1940†							
Mansfield Town 09	250	X	X	X	X	90	3170	1710‡						
Mansfield Woodhouse 10	50	X	X	X	X	5	80	30‡	2870					
Shirebrook West 11	30	X	X	X	X	X	20	20	990	40				
Langwith 12	X	X	X	X	X	X	10	30	220	X	X			
Elmton and Cresswell 13	40	X	X	X	X	X	X	X	X	94	94	219		
Whitwell 14	X	X	X	X	X	X	X	X	X	10	X	X	308	
Worksop 15	170	X	X	X	X	15	5	545	60	23	73	4059	1820	

service were in operation, British Rail could use their freedom to fix fares to experiment with the structure and possibly increase some charges.

The aggregate totals obtained by multiplying the passenger journeys in Table 13.1 by half bus return fares are as follows:

	per week	per annum
1. Weekdays only – revenue for all flows shown in Table 13.1	£2793	£145,236
2. Weekdays only – revenue excluding flows calculated from $\frac{2}{5}$ of bus riding	£2685	£139,620
3. Revenue including Saturdays if Saturday = 1 weekday	£3352	£174,304
4. Revenue including Saturdays if Saturday = $\frac{1}{2}$ weekday	£3072	£159,744
5. Revenue including Saturdays if Saturday = $\frac{1}{4}$ weekday	£2932	£152,464

The service was costed by applying typical diesel multiple unit (D.M.U.) costs to likely mileages. We worked out a hypothetical timetable to see what mileages we could cover on this route with two D.M.U. sets and with three sets, and aggregated our costs from this basic data. A key assumption was that the line remained open for freight traffic (this was not in question at the time) and consequently track costs arose only from additional maintenance to raise track to passenger standards.

Route costings were based on the following assumptions:[1]

1. Additional track maintenance required for passenger working on the route at £500 per mile = £16,000 p.a.

2. Costs of maintaining 15 unstaffed halts at £500 each p.a. = £7500 p.a.
Total overheads p.a. = £23,500.

[1] These costings were derived from data published in the British Railways Board Report, *The Reshaping of British Railways* (H.M.S.O., 1963) and related to 1968 cost levels with the help of British Railways. It should be noted that the marginal approach to track costs gives significantly lower costs than the formula used by the Ministry of Transport in assessing the amount of subsidy to be paid for grant-aided services; see Ministry of Transport, *Railway Policy*, Cmnd 3439 (H.M.S.O., 1967).

Annual fixed costs

1. Maintenance, stabling and servicing,
   provision for renewal and interest   £5700 p.a.
2. Driver and conductor guard – 2 sets of men
   per D.M.U. set and spare cover   £5500

                                             £11,200

Total Annual Charges

1. Overheads and 2 D.M.U.s   £45,900
2. Overheads and 3 D.M.U.s   £57,000

Running Costs

Maintenance, fuel and lubricants – cost per mile 1s. 10d.[1]

Using these figures we costed five possible combinations of service. As population and traffic flows were less on the northern section of the route between Mansfield and Worksop, we costed possible services which terminated at Mansfield or gave this section of the route greater frequencies.

It can be seen that none of the frequencies possible with two D.M.U. sets is very good. However, a number of permutations within the average frequency are possible in order to give above-average frequencies for morning and evening work journeys and lower frequencies in the middle of the day. Obviously the frequencies achieved have an important bearing on the proportion of potential rail traffic attracted to the service. This question could have been investigated further had the proposition to reopen the line been pursued.

The revenue estimates had been analysed in terms of potential revenue. The survey had identified users who could benefit from a transfer. It could not tell us how many would in fact choose to transfer, especially in cases where passengers have the choice of a faster rail journey as against a more frequent bus service. We dealt with this problem in two ways: first, by taking the potential total and noting the proportions of that revenue required to cover the costs of the rail service; second, by applying a crude probability factor to each of the passenger flows.

[1] All money values in this case study are expressed in old currency units, as the study took place before decimalisation.

This was based on a statistical assumption that passengers would arrive at random over time, and on the assumption that they would choose whichever form of transport provided the earlier arrival at their destination. Thus a thirty-minute rail service would pick up more potential passengers if the competing bus frequency were twenty minutes than if it were ten minutes.[1]

Table 13.2 showed that the potential revenue along the route was around £3000 per week, and this excluded generated traffic and traffic on flows only partially recorded or omitted. Table 13.3 shows that costs might range from £1200–£1700 per week.

Thus if a rail service could attract half of the potential revenue it would be able to cover its costs. If it attracted only a quarter of potential revenue, it would lose about £750 per week or just over £39,000 per annum. When the statistical probability formula was applied to the flows on Table 13.1 at the appropriate bus frequencies, the results showed that one-third of the potential revenue would be attracted.

Thus the financial calculations showed:

(a) the possibility that the line could cover its costs in the event that the proportion transferring was favourable;
(b) a very high probability that any losses would be contained within the range of £10,000 to £26,000 per annum depending on the particular service frequency chosen. The low probability estimate of attracting only a quarter of potential passengers showed that the likely losses would not be more than around £40,000 per annum.

The probability of only small losses was reinforced by the degree of underestimation in the survey already noted together with the fact that no allowance had been made for generated traffic.

The social evaluation was confined to a measurement of time

[1] The formula used was:

$$\left(\frac{\text{Minutes time savings by rail/bus}}{60} \times \text{No. of trains per hour} \right)$$
$$+ \left(\frac{\text{Interval between buses}}{60} \times \frac{\text{No. of trains per hour}}{2} \right).$$

TABLE 13.3
Costs of service

	per annum	per week
(a) 2 D.M.U. sets doing 15 round trips Nottingham–Worksop (average frequency 1¼ hours)	£73,372	£1411
(b) 2 D.M.U. sets: one set 8 round trips to Worksop; one set 10 round trips to Mansfield (average frequency Nottingham–Mansfield 1 hour with some 30-min. gaps in the peak period; average frequency Mansfield–Worksop 2½ hours)	£70,304	£1352
(c) 2 sets working a service Nottingham–Mansfield only; about 20 round trips a day, average frequency 45 mins.	£59,332	£1141
(d) 3 sets, 1 doing 8 round trips Nottingham–Worksop and 2 sets doing 18 round trips Nottingham–Mansfield (average frequency Nottingham–Mansfield 33 mins.; Mansfield–Worksop 2½ hours)	£89,492	£1721
(e) As for combination (c), but working 15 trips only to give the 45 mins. frequency in the peak period only	£60,528	£1164

savings. We proceeded as for revenue by estimating the total potential time savings available to the total possible passenger flows. The proportion of possible time savings which would accrue would be the same as the proportion of passengers who diverted to rail. First the table of time savings of rail over bus journeys on each flow was multiplied by the number of potential passengers as shown in Table 13.1 and valued at 3s. and 5s. per hour. This gave the total valuation as follows:

1. If all time is valued at 3s. per hour (the rate then used by the Ministry of Transport), this gives:
   £853 per week and £44,356 per annum.
2. If all time is valued at 5s. per hour (a rate more in line with those used in published academic cost–benefit calculations), this gives:
   £1419 per week and £73,788 per annum.

Total potential time savings would be increased by generated traffic and allowance for underestimation. However, as with potential revenue, only a proportion of these savings would actually accrue depending on the proportion of potential traffic which is attracted. If half the traffic is attracted, time savings would be worth £22,178–£36,894 p.a. If only a quarter of the traffic is attracted, the time savings would be worth £11,984–£18,447 p.a.

Potential revenue is estimated at around £3000 per week. Costs would range from £1200 to £1700 per week. If half the potential revenue could be attracted, the services would probably cover their cost.

Half the value of potential time savings would be £22,000–£37,000 per annum and provide a good 'social justification' for taking this risk.

If only one-third of potential revenue were attracted, then losses of £10,000–£26,000 p.a. might be expected. This might be a manageable size for local authority subsidy. The measurable benefits in time savings would be in the range £15,000–£25,000 so that the subsidy would be a little less than measured social benefits. Given the existence of intangible benefits of positive but unquantified value, the subsidy could be justified.

However, if only a quarter of the potential revenue were attracted, then losses of around £40,000 per annum might be incurred. This would be well in excess of measured time savings of £11,000–£18,000 per annum and a subsidy could only be justified if the intangible benefits were thought to be worth around £30,000 per annum to the local community or the national economy.

The study provided a reasonable expectation of a manageable loss well justified by social benefits. Had the local authorities been willing to make a contribution from the rates, it would have provided a good basis for asking British Rail to consider an experimental reopening of services for, say, six months at a likely cost to the local authorities of between £5000 and £13,000 and in adverse circumstances a possible cost of no more than £20,000.

PROBLEMS OF APPLICATION

The major difficulty was that the rail service studied had already been closed. Its potential passengers were dispersed over small segments of forty possible bus routes. Had the line still been open, data of passenger flows and revenues could have been easily obtained from ticket analysis or riding the trains. The preparation of the survey and organisation of the interviews was laborious and time-consuming. The length of the line and poor communications meant that interviewers required rather complicated transport schedules of their own, and paying for their travel time and transport was a significant part of the survey cost.

VARIANTS

Any rail or bus service whose withdrawal is being considered could be studied without meeting the particular problems of this study. It would normally only be worth looking at a line which is still open for freight traffic and for which it would be plausible to use marginal costing for track costs.[1] It is most improbable that any lines already closed or proposed for closure would have such bouyant passenger traffic that they could cover full track costs even where significant social benefits exist. Many railway lines were closed, especially prior to 1966, in the light of losses based on the costs of steam traction and staffed stations, and it may be that a possible case for reopening could be established with costings based on D.M.U. operations and unstaffed halts. However, routes which have already been closed are unlikely to be in areas which would qualify for government subsidies under the 1968 Transport Act, and the project could have practical significance only where local authorities might contemplate underwriting a potential loss for British Rail. There have recently been some cases of local authorities financing the extra costs of reopening a particular station and slowing a through-train to make an additional stop there. A simpler and much more manageable variant of our study might be to evaluate this kind of proposition for a station which serves an area with poor bus services. Potential passengers could be more easily identified at a particular point on a

[1] The Ministry of Transport formula for costing grant-aided services would include an allocated share of joint costs, and not just marginal track costs. However, marginal costs are relevant for deciding whether or not a service should be withdrawn and for examining the case for partial local authority subsidies.

route and some quantification of the costs and benefits involved might be helpful in showing whether a campaign to reopen a station was well advised.

FURTHER READING

There are a number of published studies applying the techniques of cost–benefit analysis to railway services which might be consulted to illustrate different approaches to this kind of exercise. These include:

G. Clayton and J. H. Rees, *The Economic Problems of Rural Transport in Wales* (University of Wales Press, 1967).

P. K. Else and M. Howe, 'Cost–Benefit Analysis and Railway Services', in *Journal of Transport Economics and Policy* (May 1969).

Ministry of Transport, *The Cambrian Coast Line: A Cost–Benefit Analysis of the Retention of Railway Services on the Cambrian Coastline* (H.M.S.O., 1969).

CHAPTER FOURTEEN

The Influence of a College on its Surroundings: Madeley

D. P. Gabriel and D. J. Hancock

INTRODUCTION

This project was undertaken by the authors with students from Madeley College of Education.

Madeley is a semi-rural village of 1100 households some five miles west of Newcastle under Lyme which is itself, geographically if not psychologically, part of the Potteries.[1] Madeley has expanded quite rapidly in the last thirty years with developments such as the building of various housing estates (council, National Coal Board and private), improvements in shopping facilities and, in 1965, the opening of Madeley College of Education. Employment opportunities in the village, excluding the college, are limited. There are two small engineering works, various farms, and the usual services; but many people, including miners, travel into the Potteries for work. In particular there are few opportunities for the employment of women. Because Madeley is relatively compact and the college such a significant feature of village life, we believed that it would be possible to isolate some of the effects on the community of such an institution. Some of the results of the investigation are outlined in this chapter in an abbreviated form, but, inevitably, this compression tends to give a rather superficial picture of some quite detailed conclusions.

AIMS

Our first aim was to give the students experience in organising and presenting an economic survey. From this work we wanted to illustrate the difficulties both in developing satisfactory

[1] The 'Potteries' delineates the Stoke on Trent area in the North Midlands, the traditional centre of the ceramics industry in the United Kingdom.

methods of investigation – e.g. using questionnaires – and in presenting a coherent set of results. Second, we hoped to show in a practical way, the injections of income and employment which can arise from siting a college in a given area. We were, at least by implication, providing useful background for understanding the multiplier. Measurement of a local multiplier would be a more difficult exercise largely because of the problem of obtaining sufficient information: it was beyond the level of the students participating and was not attempted. Third, we wanted to examine the impact which the college has made, and could make, in improving local amenities. This was to be linked with the general argument that greater use could be made by communities of existing facilities in schools and colleges. Also, with many of our students certain to be involved in the expanding field of integrated studies, there was an obvious advantage in using part of the survey to relate economics to other social sciences. Lastly, we wished to discover the attitude of villagers towards the college by using an opinion survey.

LEVEL AND REQUIREMENTS

The survey was conducted by first-year students most of whom had come straight from school. Clearly a survey of this type could be carried out by students at various levels both in colleges and schools depending on the amount of time which can be allocated and the degree of supervision. In our case the survey took four and a half days from introduction to printing the report and we were fortunate in having a week set aside for field work at the end of the college year. We deliberately decided to restrict the survey to what could be done within a week and to involve the students in every decision. Nevertheless the advantage of the survey is that it could be spread over a number of weeks or, alternatively, limited to even fewer categories than the ones we investigated. The expense of the survey was minimal, apart from paper and the use of a duplicator, because we had no major transport costs.

NECESSARY PREPARATORY WORK

The whole success of any kind of case study rests on the preparatory work. It is essential that the aims should be clearly established and rigidly adhered to. In particular, the aims should not be over-ambitious or the results will become too unwieldy. The aims have to be translated into specific areas of investigation and here it is useful to give careful guidance to avoid enthusiasm running riot. In our survey it was decided, after much discussion, to concentrate on five areas: employment of villagers in the college; the importance of lodgings; village use of college amenities; the impact of students' spending power on village services; village opinion about the college.

Once the students had decided on a definition of Madeley – the postal area – we divided the class into five groups, one for each of the areas of investigation, each group to be responsible for drawing up questionnaires, interviewing, and presenting results. Groups appointed their own chairmen and secretaries who helped to ensure co-operation among the groups and with ourselves. The questionnaires were a major problem for the students. They had to be succinct, relevant and capable of producing clear answers. Some ambiguous questions were left in and produced answers which were impossible to tabulate. At this stage we encouraged the students to try the questions on each other and this enabled them to see where many of the weaknesses lay. Finally the completed questionnaires were presented to the whole class for observations, but in fact few changes were made.

The final drafts were printed so that each person interviewed would have his replies recorded separately. We emphasised the need to ask questions properly and record accurately – not so easy when faced with busy shopkeepers or when the questioners and respondents are standing in a drizzle. The students were told not to hand out questionnaires but to make certain that they controlled the interview and to make appointments when they wished to meet specific people. They were given maps and letters of identification – vital in any situation when the public are being interviewed. The police had already been told that the survey would take place. It was left to the groups to determine the allocation of students, but we suggested that for interviews outside the college it was best to go in pairs. At the end of a very busy first day the students were ready to take the survey on to the streets.

The students worked for one and a half to two days obtaining information and the rest of the week was spent compiling the report. The summary below indicates the approach to each section of the report.

1. *Employment.* We narrowed this down to three questions: whether the job opportunities in the college had persuaded anyone to come and live in Madeley; how many college employees had not worked before the college opened; to what extent had the college caused people to switch jobs? Virtually all the interviewing took place on college premises with much of the basic information coming from the Domestic Bursar. As might be expected, the biggest impact of the college was in providing work for those who could not previously find any. This applied especially to married women for whom there were few openings in the village and prohibitive bus fares into the Potteries where wages for women are, in any case, very low.

2. *Approved lodgings.* Because the students were not permitted to interview the landladies, most of the information had to be obtained from the Lodgings Officer. It emerged that villagers received over £9000 per annum for boarding students – a substantial supplement to the low earning power of many of these families. This part of the survey emphasised that the college provided employment for women with young children for whom no employment opportunities had hitherto existed.

3. *Village use of college amenities.* Madeley is not over-blessed with social amenities either cultural or recreational, and it might be assumed that the college could help to remedy this. We decided to find out the existing contribution of the college, problems which had arisen, and whether the use of amenities could, and should, be extended. Information and opinions were gleaned from college departments. We found that some facilities – e.g. the hall, gymnasium and playing fields – were of considerable benefit to outside groups and especially the swimming pool which was used extensively by schools, youth organisations and the disabled. The real value of this part of the investigation was that it illustrated the more general problem of the utilisation of the expensive social capital invested in schools and colleges.

4. *Student spending power and village services.* Madeley has the

usual retail outlets and a questionnaire was used to examine student tastes and the spending power of both students and college employees; the importance for traders of college contracts; whether or not the presence of the college had been a factor in bringing new shops to the area. Interviews took place with shop owners and managers – the students having been warned not to be fobbed off with the newest shop assistant – but accurate information was difficult to get. The usual claim was either that figures were not available or that they would take too long to compute. Some managers appeared to assume that, in spite of identification, the students could be part of some unspecified bureaucratic plot.

5. *Village opinion on the college.* This last part of the survey was designed more to show students the problems involved in constructing an opinion survey, especially sampling, than to obtain an accurate poll of village attitudes. If we had wanted that we would hardly have used students. However, in our search to find out whether or not we had qualified for some acceptance we were pleasantly surprised, although, as might be expected, we found that we were probably welcome more for our economic benefits than for ourselves.

PROBLEMS OF APPLICATION

In addition to the problems already mentioned, there are others which take a more general form. If the work is allocated on a group basis great care must be taken to be as flexible as possible so that work can be rearranged. A just division of labour on a new project is difficult to achieve. This same problem exists within groups and a balance is necessary between the over-active chairman who trusts no one and the artful delegator who misses out himself.

In the final reports we were anxious to encourage the students to use a variety of methods to present their material. However, we found knowledge of these elementary techniques more limited than we had assumed and it would be very advisable to revise them before the survey starts.

The last problem we faced is difficult to overcome. In the first flush of enthusiasm for organising a survey it can be too easily assumed that information is non-controversial and easy to obtain when in fact it is regarded as confidential. In our case

148

it meant that some of our aims could not be achieved satisfactorily because of a lack of sufficient information on which to base any valid conclusions.

VARIANTS

The essence of this project was that we could isolate some of the consequences of placing the college in Madeley because the community is quite small. The issues we chose might have been expanded and they were not the only ones worthy of study – e.g. an investigation could be held into labour turnover and we could have tried to examine the potential implications of equal pay in causing women to switch from college work to industry in the Potteries.

Although the impact of a school might be less than a residential college, it would still make a viable study. Certainly it might include employment of teachers, domestic staff (cleaners, cooks, etc.), school contracts, and even the impact of pupil spending power. With some groups it might be better to concentrate on the provision of amenities and extend the subject to include a study of local government structure and finance. There is scope in this type of case study to adopt a variety of approaches and the work can be geared towards economics or towards a mixture of economics and other disciplines. Where possible the results of such a study should be compared with other empirical studies and any differences in conclusions analysed; for example, this study could be compared with E. K. Grime and D. N. M. Starkie, 'New Jobs for Old: An Impact Study of a New Factory in Furness', in *Regional Studies*, II, 1 (Sep 1968). Apart from their value in developing understanding of the strengths and weaknesses of different methods of economic investigations, such comparisons serve as a warning against the temptation to generalise from individual case studies.

CHAPTER FIFTEEN

Economics Field Studies for Schools

This chapter brings together three economics field studies undertaken in recent years by different schools. The authors, who have been responsible for implementing as well as writing about these studies, have been asked to restrict their account to a brief outline, as the studies have much in common and Chapter 5 of this volume, which should be read in conjunction with this chapter, considers in general terms the value of field studies in teaching economics. But there are significant differences in objective and in some of the details of preparation and organisation, and the editors hope that the comparisons, as well as the individual accounts, will be of interest and help to other teachers who may themselves decide to develop field studies; thus, for example, whilst two of the studies are undertaken by individual schools, the other is a co-operative venture by two schools in different parts of the country visiting each other's region.

One of the studies is of the Potteries; the other two are of the North-east of England.

I. *The Potteries*

Paul G. Cox

AIMS

The 'Potteries' provides a precisely defined industrial area both geographically – the coal basin of the North Staffordshire Coalfield – and industrially through the concentration of the ceramic industry within the conurbation of Stoke on Trent. The field study attempted both to examine the area as a whole, including its development, and to study firms concerned with the production of ceramic products.

Level and Requirements

The project was carried out by a group of fourteen students and two staff. The study comprised four and a half days of field work, one full day preparing reports and four or five evening sessions of discussions and report writing.

Students each had a copy of Burrows' 'Stoke-on-Trent' 1:100,000 map and group equipment included 1-in., 2½-in. and 6-in. Ordnance Survey maps[1] and drawing materials and paper suitable for wall charts. A minibus was used for transport.

Necessary Preparatory Work

Accommodation – single study-bedrooms, full board and lecture rooms – was obtained from Keele University (where the Registrar requires up to one year's notice for bookings).

Preliminary letters had to be written to firms in the area six months in advance; confirmatory letters within one month of the field work. During the term before the field work, regular weekly sessions were held with the students to discuss aims and methods of study, to compose the questionnaires to be sent to firms in advance, and to draw outlines of maps and charts.

Letters of programme, insurance details, etc., had to be sent to parents and the local education office notified about insurance and grants.

The Case Study

1. *The programme:*

Day 1   Afternoon   Arrival at Keele University.
        Evening   Background lecture by member of University.
Day 2   Morning   Group visit – Barratts Ltd, Burslem.
        Afternoon   Group visit – (*a*) Shelton Iron and Steel Works;
                                  (*b*) Goldendale Iron Company.

[1] 1:63,360 (1 in.) Sheet 110; 1:25,000 (2½ in.) Sheets SJ84, SJ85; 1:10,560 (6 in.) Sheets SJ84NW, SJ84NE, SJ84SE, SJ85SW, SJ85SE, SJ94SW, SJ94NW.

Day 2	Evening	Groups make reports:
		Group A 10 students plus staff.
		Group B 5 students plus staff.
Day 3	Morning	Group visit – Royal Doulton Ltd.
	Afternoon	Group visit – Johnson Bros. (Hanley) Ltd.
	Evening	Summarise production processes of pottery industry; compare firms visited.
Day 4	Morning and Afternoon	Survey of the distribution of the ceramic industry within the Potteries by students working in pairs.
Day 5	Afternoon	Land-use survey of Trent and Mersey, and Caldon canals.
Day 6	Morning and Afternoon	Interviews by students to gain more detailed information: (a) of firms; (b) of the area as a whole, its changes and potential.
	Evening	Reports on interviews.
Day 7	All day	Correlation of field work; preparation of field report.
Day 8		Depart from Keele University.

2. *The questionnaire*, submitted to firms, sought information on the history of the firm, its capital structure and current sources of finance, the factors affecting its location, its sources of raw materials, aspects of its labour force including labour costs, its management structure, its marketing techniques, relationship between costs and output, pricing policy and profitability.

3. *The pottery industry* provided a particularly valuable study for students taking economic history with economics. Walking the streets of the six towns of the Potteries revealed much evidence of the history of the pottery industry – potkilns of various shapes and sizes in ruin, no longer used or preserved as part of the industrial archeology of the area.

At Etruria (Hanley), an early example of an industrial village estate, the home of Josiah Wedgwood remains and now houses the offices of the Shelton Iron and Steel Company. The remains of the factory show[1] the usual features of the architecture of pottery factories – built around a courtyard with the kilns

---

[1] The building has now been razed to the ground.

towards the back, the roof crowned by a cupola and access to the courtyard by way of a great doorway. By contrast modern pottery factories are much like any other modern factories. The change in architecture is a result of the change in production techniques.

The production processes, past and modern, can be discovered by visiting the factories named in the programme. Kilns are no longer coal-fired; oil-, gas- and electric-fired kilns are favoured by different firms. From the visits, the technical language of the industry can be learnt and comparisons between firms made in the utilisation of capital equipment and labour. It is worth visiting the three potteries named in the order shown. Barratts Ltd produces utility-quality goods and demonstrate clearly the paternalistic attitude of many pottery firms, which may help to explain the good labour relations found in the area, which boasts that there has not been a strike in the pottery industry for sixty years. Royal Doulton Ltd produces fine-quality ware, both tableware and figurines. Labour costs are higher than at Barratts. Johnson Bros. (Hanley) Ltd has several factories in the Potteries, and that at Foxley Bridge is as fully mechanised as possible.

Other than the chinaware and earthenware factories there are also tileries, pipe-makers, industrial porcelain factories and the firms that make and supply the tools for the industry. They present the complex structure of the industry in the area. A necessary part of the study of the area as a whole is to find an explanation for the growth of the industry in this concentrated area and to examine the present position and possible future trends.

4. *Other industries* include coal mining and iron and steel, long established in the Potteries. While the fortunes of the coal industry in the past decade have been very mixed, production at Shelton Iron and Steel Works has been expanding with a large investment programme which made it one of Europe's most modern plants with its Kaldo convertors and continuous hot-strip mills. Marshland had been filled in with slag to form a solid platform for this part of the works (an interesting example of low opportunity cost of land). Other metal-working factories in the area include the long-established Goldendale Iron Works which still uses furnaces erected in the middle of the last century, and a brass foundry at Hanley.

Apart from the service industries to be expected in an urban concentration such as the Potteries, other industries were not represented until recently, except for Michelin Tyre Company which began operations in the mid-thirties. (It is not possible to visit this factory for industrial security reasons.) English Electric have opened a new factory, to the north of the area at Kidsgrove, influenced by the land available with government development permission, and a source of labour in an area of good industrial relations.

PROBLEMS OF APPLICATION

Permission to go down a mine was refused and some firms were unable to complete the questionnaire. Without private transport it would have been impossible to have carried out the field study as outlined and to have taken full advantage of the opportunities offered.

Factory visits would prove difficult with larger groups; most firms prefer about ten people and it is always difficult for members of larger groups to hear the guide.

II. *The North-east*

D. N. Eltringham

AIMS

The field study described in this section took place during the week ending 1 April 1966 and was the beginning of an association between the William Morris Senior High School, Walthamstow (East London), and the County Grammar School, Blyth (Northumberland). The association originated in the belief that two groups of sixth-form students living in areas economically different would benefit if they were jointly to study each other's areas. The two-year cycle of sixth-form studies would allow for the study of each area on alternate years.

More specifically the aims were to provide an opportunity to study applications of economic principles; to examine a cross-section of industrial activity in North-east England and compare it with that of the country as a whole; and to examine government policy on regional development as it applied to the North-east.

154

The students from Blyth Grammar School who took part in the study were the first- and second-year economics sixth and a business studies group. For a sufficiently comprehensive study of the area a week was felt to be essential. The choice of the last week of the spring term minimised the dislocation of the school timetable and ensured that the first-year sixth and the business studies group had studied economics for two terms, while the second-year sixth were not too close to 'A'-level examinations.

NECESSARY PREPARATORY WORK

The preparations began the previous November and were divided into three phases.

The first phase included obtaining the support of the head-master and the permission of the local education authority; arrangements for accommodating the Walthamstow party (satisfactorily completed with the aid of the Tyneside Chamber of Commerce and the Anglican Youth Training Centre at Wallsend on Tyne); and the drafting of a programme.

Lists of firms and organisations were drawn up to permit a study both of the older industries traditional to the area and of the government development policy and the newer industries introduced by it. Individual letters, not duplicated, but using a basic framework, were sent to the Personnel or Training Officers of over twenty firms. To ensure that groups visiting firms were in sufficiently small units to derive real benefit, the letters listed particular areas of activity, such as personnel, research, marketing, distribution, which pupils wished to study and from which the firm was asked to choose three. The initial letters were generally followed by a telephone discussion of the particular areas for study.

The second phase of the preparations was concerned with finalising the programme of visits and bringing the students more fully into the preparation, although they had also taken part in earlier discussions. They were now allocated in sets to particular areas of study and given the task of compiling information on their topics. For example, those concerned with personnel activity were to report on features such as the number of trade unions represented in the firm, the turnover of labour

155

and the proportion of skilled to unskilled workers. The members of the Upper Sixth were allocated the task of describing the industrial structure of Blyth. Their work was to include the changing pattern of sea traffic of the port, the rise and decline of the Blyth collieries and the growth of 'light' industries in Blyth, and was to be presented in the form of a symposium to be given in the evening of 28 March (the first day of the study).

Costs had to be finalised, meal arrangements made and a coach hired. Costs were kept down to student contributions of £1 each with the aid of a similar sum from the School Fund.

The third phase was the finalising of evening activities. As Blyth is a day school and the students were exploring their home area, attendance at evening activities was voluntary and functions therefore had to be made attractive.

THE CASE STUDY

Programme

Day and date	Morning	Afternoon	Evening
Monday 28 March	Vickers-Armstrongs (Engineering) Ltd.	River Trip. From the five bridges to Tynemouth.	Discussion period.
Tuesday 29 March	*North East Trading Estate Ltd, Gateshead.	Consett Iron and Steel Company.	Social.
Wednesday 30 March	*Colliery visits: (a) Blyth; (b) Ashington.	Swan Hunter, shipbuilders.	Dinner.
Thursday 31 March	*(a) North-East Development Council; (b) Newcastle upon Tyne Chamber of Commerce; (c) Department of Economic Affairs.	Killingworth New Town.	Theatre.
Friday 1 April	Kirkley Hall Farm Institute, Northumberland.	Free time in Newcastle.	Social and buffet supper.

* For these visits the party had to be divided into two or three groups.

Pursuit of the Aims

The attempt to see a cross-section of the industry of the North-east is indicated by the programme. Government policy of regional development in the area was studied by visiting four organisations directly concerned with this task. The lack of co-operation among these organisations, sometimes bordering on competition, rather surprised the group. However, ample

156

opportunity was given to discuss the problems facing the area and to debate possible solutions to these problems. The visit to Killingworth was chosen as an example of Northumberland County Council's 'new towns'.

The aim of applying certain economic principles was accomplished in several ways, for example:

(a) *Capital.* The river trip down the Tyne showed the capital requirement for shipping – from small quay-loading cranes to dry docks. The distinction between fixed and circulating capital was clearly made at Broadlow Farm, part of the Kirkley Hall Institute.

(b) *Diversification within the firm.* At Vickers we visited a shop engaged in the construction of heavy tanks, another shop making curtain rails, and yet another making moulds for bodies of a popular children's pedal car. One of the students suggested a motto for the firm: 'You name it; we'll make it.' At Swan Hunters we went through the joinery shops and saw ships' furniture being made; also we found out that the firm has supplied furniture to various hotels and had recently completed a contract to supply furniture to one of the country's new universities.

(c) *Specialisation.* At the Universal Bedding Company (part of Great Universal Stores) we saw twenty separate tasks in manufacturing a mattress.

(d) *Interdependence of firms.* At Consett Iron Company we saw steel plate marked for Swan Hunters, and a machine that had been supplied by Vickers, made with steel from Consett. The turbines in the power house were from Parsons, a Tyneside firm.

Presentation of Work

Scheduling the field study for the last week of term allowed individual work to be written up during the Easter holiday. The work was presented at the beginning of the summer term and the first half of the term was allowed for collation, editing and typing.

The association between Blyth Grammar School and William Harris School, at the time of writing, is in its fifth year. In 1970 a field study similar to that of 1966 has been planned.

III. *Tyneside and West Durham*
Brian R. G. Robinson

AIMS

The basic aim was to enable sixth-form students to see more of
the real world of economics, and to try to test, sometimes
rigorously, sometimes in a more elementary way, some theories
and policies to a greater depth than can be done in textbooks.
This was to be done by factory visits, by meeting representatives
of business, unions and regional/local organisations, and by
making surveys in the economic region chosen for study. A
theme was taken for the economic region studied, i.e. economic
problems of a development area, and study was to be made of
aggregate demand there, of labour mobility and industrial
relations policies, as well as of the theories of pricing, wages,
profits and industrial location. A week was needed for the
course, because each day's experience is built upon the previous
day's, and at the end of a week's regional field study the student's cumulative experience is greater than if he did field work
for a day per week for five or six weeks.

LEVEL AND REQUIREMENTS

These courses at Brockenhurst Grammar School (Hampshire)
were organised usually for lower sixth-form students towards
the end of the academic year. It would have been inappropriate
to our purpose for them to begin field study work until they had
mastered the elementary theoretical work and studied some
general applied economics. At sixth-form age the student has in
theory, and it seems also in practice, reached the stage when, as
Piaget[1] points out, he can make intelligent generalisations of his
own from a number of given instances. Such is the very kernel
of the survey techniques and industrial visits work involved in
the field study. There is probably a place for field work, to see
the practical work of economics more fully, with fourth- and
fifth-year pupils, but they would not have reached the stage
where they could generalise from a particular set of facts.

[1] B. Inhelder and J. Piaget, *The Growth of Logical Thinking* (London, 1958).

158

The preparatory work for the course chosen for this case study, Tyneside and West Durham Region (April 1967), was similar to that for previous courses undertaken by Brockenhurst Grammar School, in South Yorkshire (1965) and in South-east Lancashire (1966): to choose first of all a convenient youth hostel and arrange accommodation, and then to write to two or three firms in major industries for visits during the week of the course. This completed, an overall plan for the course was drawn up including all other visits, and the organisations and firms were then contacted with suggestions for a specific date and time of visit. The co-operation of management, union and local/regional organisations is difficult to overpraise; few alterations had to be made to the plan. A local coach was booked for transport to and from the study region, and when the overall plan had been fully agreed with firms and organisations a West Durham coach was hired for transport in the study area.

The earlier courses, originating with an idea by the Headmaster, Dr L. R. Wood, were joint courses in economics and geography, with economics predominating. The lengthened 1967 course contained still more economics (since geography field centres ran pure geography courses) and was a four-day-plus integrated economics course, with one day of physical geography remaining largely unintegrated. The sixth form of nearly 400, with over 100 studying economics, provided a large student body from which to draw. Before the course the twenty-four students going to Tyneside did preparatory work on industries and organisations to be visited, and this work, together with details of firms and local towns prepared by the two staff, formed a scheme of preliminary background notes for the course. This written work was oriented towards the theme of the course, 'The Economic Problems of Development Districts', to add special purpose and interest to the work.

The course was based at Edmundbyers Youth Hostel, which has good facilities for discussion and written work, six miles west of Consett. One of the basic aims of the course was to try to test macro-economic theory at work; to find out whether the capital expenditure of government on roads and on attracting new industry by grants, etc., to the region was mopping up unemployment caused by declining industries in the area. Visits were made to a shipyard and a coal-mine, and at both management were asked questions about redundancies, and the industry where workers were re-employed, as well as questions about pricing, wages, profits and industrial location to test other theories. Science-based industry and light engineering firms received similar general scrutiny and the students tried to find out from where they drew labour. Statisical surveys were made of Consett and Byker (a residential area near the shipyards of Newcastle) to discover whether the unemployed and those fearing redundancy could be re-employed in growth industries locally. The party wrote essays after the course and held discussion sessions on and after the course, out of which they produced a 48-page booklet.

THE CASE STUDY

Tyneside and West Durham: The Economic Problems of Development Areas (April 1967)

		Morning	Afternoon	Evening
Sun	9 April	Brockenhurst to Edmundbyers (brief survey of Bishop Auckland).		
Mon	10 April	Physical Geography on Carboniferous Limestone (West Durham).		
Tue	11 April	Walker Shipyard, Newcastle.	Microwave Ltd, Shiremoor.	Talk by Divisional Organiser, A.E.U.
Wed	12 April	Socio-economic-geographical survey of Consett.		
Thur	13 April	Whitburn Colliery	Free afternoon in Durham City.	Consett Steelworks.
Fri	14 April	Team Valley Trading Estate.	(1) Employment survey of Byker. (2) N.E.D.C.* talk and discussion.	Free evening in Newcastle.
Sat	15 April	Edmundbyers to Brockenhurst.		

* North-East Development Council.

PROBLEMS OF APPLICATION

A difficulty on factory visits was that guides were usually technically biased and students needed to be carefully briefed beforehand on the sort of economics questions to ask. A problem in survey work was that during the day many workers were not at home, but on a more recent course when we did this work during the evening there were just as many out – this time in the bingo hall! We have found that with considerable preparation and follow-up the students do not become confused by looking at the real world of economics, but the practical work strongly reinforces their understanding of theory, and puts them ahead of the latest applied economics textbooks in information on some aspects of recent economic change. It is difficult for small economics sixth forms to do field studies on their own, but groups of schools could combine for this purpose, or economics staff of the local college of education could, perhaps, organise a course for local schools, such as Worcester College of Education has done for West Midlands schools since 1968.[1]

One of the most important academic conclusions of the course is summed up in the preface to the students' booklet, '. . . that, due to the insufficient quantity of flat land for major industrial development in West Durham, labour in declining trades should be encouraged by much more positive and expensive means to move into the newer industries being established in the east of the county'. One of the most important educational conclusions of the course was that the average and less able students did better work than usual on the course, and in school classwork after it; the course, by its emphasis on the practical world of economics, had created a new and persistent interest in the subject. The field study had helped these students in economics in the same way as Nuffield practical work has helped students of physical science.

[1] M. Day and B. R. G. Robinson, 'Combined Schools Field Studies in Economics: Organization and New Techniques', *Economics* (forthcoming).

CHAPTER SIXTEEN

Investing on the Stock Exchange
C. T. Sandford

Two case studies (with variants) are considered in this chapter. The first is a role-playing study in which the student acts as a stock exchange investor, undertakes imaginary investments in stocks and shares, and observes and records what happens to his purchases. It is therefore necessarily limited to the period of the student's course in economics, and must therefore be confined to an examination of short- and medium-term fluctuations in stocks and shares.

The second study is a project relating to the progress of investments over a longer period of time, to attempt to explore the factors affecting trend movements in the prices of stocks and shares.

The two studies have some general aims in common. Many students, especially those from working-class homes, find the stock exchange an alien world whose business is conducted in a foreign language. The exercises therefore serve to familiarise the student with the stock market, its wares, its method of operation and its terminology.

The studies can also serve as a peg on which to hang a number of related discussions, such as the functions of the stock exchange, the characteristics of different forms of business enterprise, the legal requirements of companies, the function of speculation in an economy. They can also provide an illustration of different market forms; the purchase and sale of shares of the industrial giants approximates to a perfect market, while there will be a high degree of imperfection in the market for the shares of a small, little-known public company. Further, a consideration of stocks and shares is, of course, a necessary adjunct to the study of interest and profit.

Beyond these general aims, the two studies each have more specific objectives.

I. SHORT- AND MEDIUM-TERM FLUCTUATIONS IN STOCKS AND SHARES

Aims

The particular aim of this study is to help the student to appreciate the nature and causes of some of the fluctuations in the prices of stocks and shares. In particular, students often find difficulty in correctly relating interest rates and security prices, and the study should help to clarify this relationship.

Level and Requirements

The study is suitable for 'A'-level students, first-year degree, H.N.C./H.N.D. in business studies and various professional courses. An appropriately simplified version can also be used with advantage for classes at lower levels, e.g. 'O'- level economics with secretarial students.

Students work on their own and any number may participate. The exercise takes place over a period of at least four months in the students' own time, but at least one teaching period is necessary at the beginning to explain the project and another at the end to discuss the results.

The only material necessary for the basic projects is regular student access to a daily or weekly newspaper (e.g. *The Economist*) giving a wide range of stock exchange quotations.

Necessary Preparatory Work

As a minimum the terminology of the project must be explained: the meaning of redeemable and irredeemable government securities, ordinary share, and so on. But it is probably preferable to discuss at the same time the functions and method of operation of the stock exchange and to give additional detail of different kinds of shares, distinguishing the characteristics of ordinary and preference shares, explaining debenture stock and illustrating different central and local government securities.

A useful supplement to the study is a visit to a stock exchange, with the opportunity to put questions to an expert; but a visit has most value at or near the end of the study rather than as a preliminary. (The Council of the London Stock Exchange encourages visitors to its public gallery, shows films about the Stock Exchange in its own cinema and also loans them free of charge to educational institutions.)

THE CASE STUDY

At the end of the preparatory discussion students are given instructions on their role as investors which may be verbal or (preferably) duplicated. The following is a slightly modified version of instructions given to a group of first-year students at Bath University.

> You are to play the role of an investor on the Stock Exchange who has come into a legacy and decides to invest in a limited number of assets of different kinds to observe their behaviour in order to systematise his experience for future investment policy.
>
> You have £4000 to invest. Ignoring costs of investment, e.g. stamp duties, brokerage fees, you are to invest as follows:
>
> 1. £1000 in a particular issue of an irredeemable government security of your choice;
> 2. £1000 in a particular issue of a redeemable government security of your choice;
> 3. £1000 in a relatively safe ordinary share of a major company (or in a particular unit trust);
> 4. £1000 in a speculative share.
>
> You are to note down the details of your investments at the date of 'purchase' and record their market price on that day. You are, further, to take regular weekly readings of the prices of your particular stocks and shares and plot these price data, for each of them, on a graph.
>
> You will 'realise' your investments just before (date of handing in) when you will calculate the value of each of your four categories of investment, assess capital gain, or loss, and compare the relative performance of the different forms of investment. You should write an account to be handed in on . . . . explaining the main fluctuations in price, and accounting for the relative performance of the different investments.

Guidance on Relevant Factors

Some price variations, especially those of ordinary shares, may defy rational analysis; but you should watch over your investments and note happenings likely to affect their price. In particular you should:

1. Record changes in Bank Rate. (Note that the expectation of a change in interest rates, as well as actual changes, will affect the price of your investments; indeed, any particular change in Bank Rate may be anticipated by the market and discounted in advance.)

2. Collect information about the companies in which you have invested, e.g. main locations, products, raw materials, markets, so that you can discern factors which may affect the profitability and hence the price of the shares (e.g. strikes affecting the firms' products or supplies; or political instability in its main markets or sources of supply). You should also record the dates and amounts of dividend payments. (Much of this detail can be obtained from the firm itself, particularly from the latest Chairman's Report.)

3. Consider the possible effects of any economic policy actions by Governments on expected profitability, e.g.
   (*a*) currency devaluations or revaluations;
   (*b*) budget changes such as changes in corporation tax; outlay tax on the firms' products or materials; and changes in government contracts or new contracts;
   (*c*) reports of government agencies such as the National Board for Prices and Incomes and the Monopolies Commission which affect the firm in which you have invested.

4. Watch out for take-over bids or rumours of take-overs.

5. See what is happening in other international stock markets, especially Wall Street.

PROBLEMS OF APPLICATION

One problem is how much detail should the teacher give by way of guidance to students about possible causes of fluctuations in the prices of stocks and shares and how much should students be left to discover for themselves? There is no hard and fast rule, and much depends on the level of the students. But the author's view is that students new to economics need the kind of broad guidance outlined above on what to watch for; this still leaves to them the discovery of the particular factors at work.

There is a particular problem of terminology in the use of 'investment'. Students new to economics have difficulty in firmly grasping the fundamental economic meaning of investment as the addition to real capital over a period of time; they think of investment solely as lending money or buying assets. To use 'investment' in this case study in this more common but less fundamental sense therefore carries the danger that their misunderstanding will be perpetuated. One way of trying to deal with the problem is to avoid the use of investment in the study and to talk instead simply of buying and selling stocks and shares. But this is unsatisfactory; the teacher may succeed in avoiding the word 'investment', but the financial columns of the press to which students are expected to refer to carry through the case study will certainly use it. It is better to grasp the nettle firmly and take advantage of the occasion to indicate the two ways in which 'investment' is used, indicating both the differences and the relationship between the meanings.

VARIANTS

There are a large number of possible variants to the study. More or less detail on possible causal factors may be given; different investment portfolios may be prescribed; or the student may be left entirely free to determine his own portfolio.

Thus a group of students may be told simply to invest so as to maximise capital gain. They can choose in what to invest and are free to change their investments, provided they register the changes through a 'broker', appointed in the class. (An essential condition to prevent back-dated changes in the light of hindsight!)[1] This variant can be used with an elementary class or on a more sophisticated basis allowing for complications such as brokerage fees and capital-gains taxes. (To allow for payment of long-term capital-gains tax, students could be given part of their allocation for investment in the form of shares which are assumed to have been in their possession from a specified date at least a year earlier.)

[1] I owe this variant to E. G. West, 'Learning by Doing: A Guildford Experiment', in *Economics* (autumn 1956).

A further alternative is to divide a class into groups, each of which constitutes a syndicate with a specified sum for investment. Each syndicate is left free to determine its own investments, but in accordance with a prescribed objective, e.g. one syndicate must seek maximum capital gain; another high-yielding assets; a third, stability of yield. This approach has the advantage that it leads naturally to a discussion of the different characteristics of various types of share and security to meet the varying needs of investors; but during the limited period likely to be available for the case study, objectives other than maximum capital gain are not very meaningful.

As an addition to playing the role of investor, students may be given a complementary project – a list of questions to which they have to find the answers from the reading arising from their surveillance of their investments, e.g. what are bulls, bears and stags? What is a cumulative preference and what is a participating preference share? What is a unit trust? And so on.

II. TREND MOVEMENTS IN THE PRICES OF STOCKS AND SHARES

AIMS

The particular aim of this project is to help the student towards an understanding of the causes and nature of longer-term trends in the prices of stocks and shares and some appreciation of their consequences, especially in inflationary conditions.

LEVEL AND REQUIREMENTS

In the comparatively simple form in which it is here presented, this project is suitable for the same students as the previous role-playing case study; but, as it requires a little more understanding of economics, it should be used later in the course. A suitable time would be after the completion of the study on short- and medium-term fluctuations in stocks and shares; as a small project, it is particularly suitable as a follow-up study.

The more sophisticated variants mentioned are only suitable for more advanced students.

Students need to have access to stock-market quotations and figures of the index of retail prices over a long period of time.

167

Useful sources are back numbers of *The Economist*, various numbers of the *Annual Abstract of Statistics*, and the series of the London and Cambridge Economics Service in *Key Statistics*, *1900–1966*.

NECESSARY PREPARATORY WORK

Students require a knowledge of stock exchange terminology, as for the previous study, and of index numbers. A study and discussion of inflation, and its consequences on the distribution of income and wealth, should precede or immediately follow the project.

THE CASE STUDY

The study of long-term movements in the capital market can be introduced in various ways, but investment for retirement provides a human interest and paints more vividly the effect of inflation on fixed incomes.

Either by individual projects, or as a joint project with particular tasks given to each member of the group, the students can be asked to consider a particular case and then to seek out the anwers to certain questions. Thus the case history might be:

A man sold up his business and retired in (say) the last week of 1948. He received £10,000 for his business, all of which, in search of a secure income, he invested in 'Consols'. Just twenty years later, in the last week of 1968, he died.

The first group of questions might relate to the real and money value of his income and capital. Thus, the students might be asked to discover the annual income he received from his investment; the money value of his investment at the time of his death; the decline in his real income and the real value of his capital by the time of death.

The second group of questions might compare the income and capital value of his investment in Consols with other forms of investment, in particular ordinary shares. Thus, the students might be asked to discover what the money and the real value of his investment would have been if, instead of investing in Consols, he had bought a portfolio of ordinary shares of which the prices changed in the same proportion as the index of
168

ordinary shares (e.g. that recorded in *Key Statistics*, supplemented for the later period by one of the *Financial Times* indices).

Finally a group of questions, for written answer or discussion, to bring out causal factors such as the move into ordinary shares as a 'hedge' against inflation; the rise in interest rates; and the subsequent establishment of interest rates at a higher level in part as a result of an inflationary psychology which leads investors to expect prices to go on rising and hence to require higher interest to offset falling money values.

VARIANTS

The dates over which the investment is held can of course be varied. In a more sophisticated version, the range of investment alternatives can be widened. Some widening can take place without presenting serious difficulties in determining the annual income or capital valuation, e.g. the inclusion of investment in the Post Office Savings Bank, or in a well-known building society. But including investment in, for example, houses or land, raises more difficult issues of obtaining and interpreting data, and is only suitable and useful for more advanced students.

CHAPTER SEVENTEEN

Aspects of the United Kingdom Balance of Payments[1]

M. K. Johnson

AIMS

The project is designed to enable students to collect and interpret official government statistics on international payments and to relate their findings to the theory of the balance of payments and to government economic policy.

The aim of the project is to study the U.K. balance of payments over a period of time, such as a decade. The use of such a time span enables students to obtain a much clearer picture of the foreign trade position, which can serve as an introduction to a discussion of the place of balance of payments considerations in overall government policy. Students can examine the trends in particular items of the balance of payments, and also observe the fluctuations which have occurred. The statistics of any particular year are put in historical perspective, and students are led to question the importance attached to, say, the monthly trade figures. Particular weaknesses can be isolated, and discussed in relation to possible government action.

LEVEL AND REQUIREMENTS

The project is suitable for various courses, depending on the amount of detail required. It can be tailored to suit 'A'-level, first- or second-year degree, H.N.D. and H.N.C. in business studies, and various professional courses.

The best source of information is the current *U.K. Balance of Payments*, but the *Annual Abstract of Statistics* can also be used for less detailed studies (both H.M.S.O).

No special materials are required.

[1] This case study is a modification of 'Aspects of the Balance of Payments – a Sixth Form Project', in *Economics*, Vol. 6, Part 3, spring 1966.

The project should be preceded by a thorough study of the balance of payments as conventionally treated in the textbooks. It could be usefully sandwiched between a descriptive study of the accounts and a study of government policy.

One teaching period would be necessary to introduce students to the source material and to allocate individual parts of the project. Each student should have a clear idea of what he is doing in relation to the others, so that he can prepare answers to questions which are likely to arise elsewhere; for example, a student working on private investment in the capital account should then be ready to link his work with that of other students working on invisible trade.

Students should then come to the next teaching period with an individual set of statistics and a written interpretation or summary of their findings. Where possible, copies should be made available to all members of the project; alternatively, slides of the statistics (and, perhaps, graphs) could be prepared for an overhead projector. A useful discussion can only take place if all members of the project have easy access to all the findings.

After the teaching period spent in collating the data, and in drawing provisional conclusions, further periods could be spent in discussion, which might be based on particular articles such as those listed below.

The Case Study

Each student is given a particular item of the balance of payments to study. For example, using the *U.K. Balance of Payments 1969*, the group could study the period 1958–67 inclusive, and work could be divided along the following lines:

Student 1: A summary of the visible balance, the invisible balance and the current balance (from Table 1).

Student 2: A study of the component items of visible trade from Tables 1 and 7).

Student 3: A study of the component items of invisible trade (from Tables 1 and 8, and perhaps later tables also).

Student 4: A summary of the current balance, the balance of long-term capital, and the balance of current and long-term capital transactions (from Table 1).

The detail required would depend on the level of the work, and the amount of time available.

The students would then report their findings at the next teaching period. For example, in a recent project of this kind, the first student provided the data shown in Table 17.1.

TABLE 17.1
U.K. visible, invisible and current balances, 1958–67

Year	1958	1959	1960	1961	1962	1963	1964	1965	1966	1967
Visible balance (£m.)	29	−117	−406	−152	−102	−80	−519	−237	−84	−566
Invisible balance (£m.)	315	260	141	148	214	194	138	187	148	286
Current balance (£m.)	344	143	−265	−4	112	114	−381	−50	64	−283

He pointed out that there had been only one visible surplus during the ten-year period, and that had been a small one. There had been an accumulated visible deficit of £2234 million. However, the U.K. had recorded a substantial invisible surplus each year, ranging from a minimum of £141 million to a maximum of £315 million. As a result, the current balance had been in deficit in only five years out of the ten (and in one of these years the deficit had been only £4 million). The accumulated invisible surplus was £2028 million, so that altogether the deficit on current account over the decade was only £206 million. Linking this with the reserves position, he pointed out that, if the current account were considered in isolation, there had been an annual drain on the reserves of only £20–21 million on average.

These data led to a discussion about the alleged 'chronic weakness' of the current account, the relative importance of visible and invisible trade and the fluctuations which took place from year to year in the trade figures. It also led to a discussion of the balance of payments in the economic history of the U.K., a topic which was returned to later.

The data provided by the fourth student were as shown in Table 17.2.

The accumulated deficit on current account was £206 million, as the first report had shown. Added to this was an accumulated long-term capital outflow of £1633 million. In only one

TABLE 17.2

U.K. current and long-term capital balances, 1958–67

Year	1958	1959	1960	1961	1962	1963	1964	1965	1966	1967
Current balance (£m.)	344	143	−265	−4	112	114	−381	−50	64	−283
Balance of long-term capital (£m.)	−196	−255	−192	68	−98	−149	−363	−202	−112	−134
Balance of current and long-term capital transactions (£m.)	148	−112	−457	64	14	−35	−744	−252	−48	−417

year was there a net capital inflow. As a result, the balance of current and long-term capital transactions was in deficit seven years out of ten, with an accumulated deficit of £1839 million. This student remarked that, until he had studied the data, he had believed that the main – if not the sole – function of the capital account was to correct any imbalance on the current account. This is an impression often left by elementary text-books, and a long-period survey of balance of payments statistics shows up the error more dramatically than does a single set of figures.

This student, in fact, suggested that the main weakness of the U.K. lay in the capital account rather than the current account, and that the Government should have taken steps to curb foreign investment to a level consonant with the current balance. If net overseas investment had been zero, he argued, the drain on the reserves would have been only about £20 million p.a. instead of about £180 million. This argument led to a discussion of the merits and demerits of foreign investment, and of the links between the capital account and the current: the stimulus to exports, and the inflow of interest, profits and dividends.

A further discussion took place with regard to the balancing item: over a period, there was an accumulated net credit of £420 million. How did this arise? What were the implications for the true deficit or surplus?

These arguments were revived at a later stage when the detailed data for the capital account were presented, the net capital outflow being divided into private investment and government lending abroad. What were the reasons for government loans? Were they strong enough to justify such a large outflow, given the state of the current account?

The following basic table (Table 17.3) was produced on invisible trade.

TABLE 17.3

Combined credits and debits on invisible account, U.K. 1958–67 (£m)

	Total credits	Total debits	Net credits
Government	439	−4054	−3615
Shipping	6762	−6833	−71
Civil aviation	1286	−1060	+226
Travel	1831	−2276	−445
Interest, profits and dividends	8207	−4735	+3472
Miscellaneous	5412	−2784	+2628
Private transfers	1175	−1342	−167

Each item was discussed in detail, and questions were asked about the trend in each item over the ten-year period. This led to criticisms of government policy towards, for example, tourism and foreign investment. Further figures were obtained from Table 10 about the large government debit, so that this could be analysed into (*a*) military, (*b*) administrative and diplomatic, and (*c*) foreign aid components.

These examples show the general outline of the project; further detailed reports were given on visible trade and monetary movements, and a final analysis of the U.K. balance of payments in this period was prepared.

It may be objected that the analysis is somewhat superficial, but it fulfils the basic aims of collecting and attempting to interpret statistics: very often, students have little or no idea of the order of magnitude of variables such as export receipts or capital outflows. How far the statistical survey can be linked with theory and government policy depends largely on the time available. Much wider reading is necessary: students could complete the project, for example, by writing an essay on a particular aspect of the balance of payments, such as the relationship between economic growth and the balance of payments.

The further reading for follow-up discussion depends very much on the level at which the project is being undertaken. Examples of useful articles are given at the end of this chapter.

PROBLEMS OF APPLICATION

The main limitation is probably the availability of data. Ideally each student should have his own copy of the source material. Where copies have to be shared, a teaching period may have to be sacrificed while students copy the basic data.

The project outlined refers to the period 1958–67. As the pound was devalued on 18 November 1967, any complicating effects of devaluation were ignored, as lying outside the period. A study of subsequent years would have to take account of devaluation.

VARIANTS

A more elaborate study could be undertaken by a comparative analysis of the balance of payments of two or more countries. Thus the reasons for the U.S.A. and the U.K. deficits could be compared.

This sort of study can easily be applied to other topics, for example national income, government revenue and expenditure. It could be particularly useful in national income studies, where the basic components could be analysed in some detail, e.g. consumption expenditure could be disaggregated into durable and non-durable; investment expenditure into housing, fixed capital, stocks, and so on.

FURTHER READING

'Which Balance of Payments?', in *Westminster Bank Review* (Nov 1965).
A. Maddison, 'How Fast Can Britain Grow?', in *Lloyds Bank Review* (Jan 1966).
W. A. P. Manser, 'Should We Close the Trade Gap?', in *Westminster Bank Review* (Feb 1966).

Note on Contributors

Joint Editors: C. T. Sandford and M. S. Bradbury

Authors

M. S. BRADBURY, a graduate in economics of London University, joined the staff of the City of London College (now part of the City of London Polytechnic) in 1964 and became a senior lecturer in 1967. Since February 1969 he has been an economic adviser at the Ministry of Transport (now Department of the Environment). He contributed to *Teaching Economics* (1967) and is a contributor to and joint editor of *Economics*.

PAUL G. COX read economics and geography and took a diploma in education at Keele University. During 1962–3 he held a Rotary International Fellowship at Ibadan University, Nigeria. Appointed to Bromley Grammar School 1963, he became head of the economics department in 1965; in January 1970 he left Bromley to head an economics department at Tonbridge School. A keen member of the Economics Association, he has held part-time tutorships in teaching methods in economics at Oxford University and Goldsmiths, College, London.

W. W. DANIEL is a Senior Research Associate at PEP (Political and Economic Planning) where he is developing a programme of research on productivity bargaining and manpower redeployment. He has been engaged in social science research in one form or another since his graduation in psychology from Manchester University in 1961. In addition to university appointments at Manchester and Bath, his career has included periods at the steel industry's management college, Ashorne Hill, and with Research Services Ltd, a commercial survey and research agency. There he led the team responsible for the research on which the PEP report on *Racial Discrimination in England* was based, and he is author of the Penguin version of that report.

176

D. N. ELTRINGHAM graduated in economics at the University of London in 1957 and has been head of the commerce and economics department, County Grammar School, Blyth, since 1958. He has been lecturing part-time at Newcastle upon Tyne Polytechnic in economics and management studies since 1961 and a tutor for Pitman Correspondence College since 1962, for whom he has written courses in economics and applied economics. He is author of *Agricultural Economics* (Ginn, 1970).

D. P. GABRIEL read for his degree of London University at the London School of Economics. After a brief period in industry he entered the teaching profession and has taught for eight years in grammar schools. He was appointed to his present post of lecturer in economics at Madeley College of Education in 1967.

D. J. HANCOCK graduated in economics and history at St Andrews University. He spent three years in industry before commencing a teaching career. After nine years in secondary schools, he was appointed to initiate the teaching of economics at Madeley College of Education and since 1969 has been head of the economics department at the College.

M. K. JOHNSON graduated B.A. Economics at Cambridge in 1960, M.A. 1964. From 1965 to 1968 he was head of the economics department at St Clement Danes Grammar School. He has been a lecturer at Hatfield Polytechnic since 1968. He is co-author with J. Harvey of *Modern Economics: Study Guide and Workbook* and of *An Introduction to Macro-economics* (Macmillan, 1969 and 1971)

MYRON L. JOSEPH, Professor of Economics and Head of the Department of Administration and Management Science at Carnegie-Mellon University (formerly Carnegie Institute of Technology), was educated at City College, New York, Columbia University and Wisconsin University. Besides university teaching he has worked as an economist in government service and is a consultant to the Council of Economic Advisers. He has written widely on his special field of labour economics. His activities and publications also show his continuing concern to improve teaching methods in economics. With Norton Seeber he has written *Workbook in Economics* (Prentice-Hall, 4th ed. 1968); with Philip Saunders he contributed 'Playing the Market Game' to *New Research in Economic Education* (ed.

K. Lumsden) (Prentice-Hall, 1970) and he is author of 'Some Different Approaches to Teaching Economics' in the *Journal of Economic Education* (spring 1970). He is a trustee of the Joint Council on Economic Education.

NORMAN LEE, who holds a Ph.D. of London University, is currently a senior lecturer in economics at the University of Manchester. He specialises in transport and industrial economics. Dr Lee edited *Teaching Economics* (Economics Association, 1967) and is the author of various articles on economics and on education in economics.

R. F. R. PHILLIPS was educated at Clifton and Trinity College, Oxford. He taught for two years at a high school in Liverpool and was assistant lecturer in education at the College of St Mark and St John, Chelsea. After five years' war service he became head of the economics department of Sutton Grammar School. He has been Secretary of the Economics Association since 1948 and contributed to *The Teaching of Economics* (1958) and to *Teaching Economics* (1967). He is moderator in economics for the Associated Examining Board. In 1969 he was awarded the O.B.E.

BRIAN R. G. ROBINSON, after graduating in 1961 at Sheffield University, studied for his diploma in education at King's College, Newcastle upon Tyne. From 1962 to 1967 he taught economics at Brockenhurst Grammar School in Hampshire where he developed economics field studies. He now teaches economics at Worcester College of Education where he has organised economics field studies for teachers and schools the West Midlands. He is currently researching for a higher degree into early socialist economic and social ideas.

MICHAEL ROSE graduated in economics and social anthropology at the University of Cambridge, and has held a variety of teaching and research posts in the Universities of Salford, Bath and Cambridge. He is at present a lecturer in the School of Humanities and Social Sciences, Bath University. He is co-author of papers on the process of 'computerisation' in industry and author of *Computers, Managers and Society* (Penguin, 1969).

C. T. SANDFORD, a graduate in economics at the University of Manchester and a history graduate of London University, became Professor of Political Economy in 1965 at the new Bath University and the first head of the School of Humanities and Social Sciences. In the summer of 1969 he was Visiting Professor in Economics and Public Finance at the University of Delaware, U.S.A. His publications on economics include *Taxing Inheritance and Capital Gains* (1965, Institute of Economic Affairs), *Taxation* (1966, Institute of Economic Affairs), *The Economics of Public Finance* (Pergamon, 1969), *Realistic Tax Reform* (Chatto & Windus/Charles Knight, 1971) and *Taxing Personal Wealth* (Allen & Unwin, 1971); his writings on education include contributions to *A Technological University: An Experiment in Bath* (1966) and *Teaching Economics* (1967). He is currently external assessor in economics for two colleges of education.

SYLVIA TRENCH was educated at Somerville College, Oxford. She graduated in P.P.E. in 1957. Mrs Trench has worked for Political and Economic Planning, the National Economic Development Office and the Department of Economic Affairs on research projects on economic growth and transport problems. She is currently lecturer in the Department of Industrial Economics at Nottingham University. Her publications include *Growth in the British Economy* with G. R. Denton; *Paying for the Railways*; *The Cost of Roads*; *Transport in the Common Market*, all published by PEP.